Fu Up Stephen's Brae

The Midmills Era at Inverness Royal Academy
1895 - 1979

by Charles Bannerman

Published on behalf of
Inverness Royal Academy
by
St Michael Publishing
Abban Street
Inverness
IV3 8HH

October, 1999

ISBN : 1 901567 09 5

---

the author

Charles Bannerman was a pupil at Inverness Royal Academy from 1965-71 before graduating in Chemistry from Edinburgh University in 1975. He has taught the subject at his old school since 1977 and is now a Senior Teacher in the department. This is his third book and in between his two works on Inverness Royal Academy, he published "Against All Odds", the official account of the formation of Inverness Caledonian Thistle FC, in 1997.

He is a regular sports broadcaster on BBC Scotland and contributor to the Inverness Courier's sports pages. His other main interest is athletics where he still attempts to keep running himself and over the years he has coached a number of international performers. His wife Dorothy is also a former pupil and his children Martin and Jenny are both pupils at the school.

Acknowledgements

My first "thank you" has to be to everyone who bought 'Up Stephen's Brae' and in particular those who contacted me to say how much they had enjoyed it. This was a great incentive to go for the sequel.

I am grateful to the school's Rector John Considine for agreeing to this publication going ahead and to our archivist Robert Preece. Without my extensive access to the archive, this book would not have been possible.

Ruth Black of St. Michael Publishing has done a marvellous job in desktop publishing and printing this volume and its visual appeal is entirely due to her. I have merely written the words and chosen the photographs whereas the presentation of this volume has been completely Ruth's. I am once again most grateful to Eddie Hutcheon for his proofreading of the text. Thanks also to Gordon Harvey on whose original design for the cover of 'Up Stephen's Brae' this latest cover has been based.

I am anticipating that the School Office will again be involved in selling this book as well as dealing with many queries about availability. I hope in anticipation that this does not disrupt an already busy office routine.

Thanks also, once again, to Malcolm Herron, manager of James Thin in Inverness who has cooperated greatly in the distribution of this book within the town and also to John MacDonald, editor of the Inverness Courier, for his permission to use extracts from the paper.

I am particularly indebted to contributors over the years to the various school magazines and log books. In addition the historical writings of the late Drs. D.J. MacDonald and Evan Barron were invaluable in the case of the earlier chapters, as were Dr. Barron's accounts of World War 1 in the three Academicals of the 1916-21 period. Thanks also to Jim Brennan and Sid Atkinson for their historical advice and to Buckie for his drawing of the Gordonstoun bell.

The other invaluable source has been individual interviews with Elizabeth Chalmers, Nancy Scott and Eddie Hutcheon. Deirdre MacLennan was good enough to provide me with a taped interview with her mother while her brother Brian Denoon wrote one of the more memorable contributions obtained from the 1992 Bicentenary Historical Folio.

My thanks also to those as yet unanticipated who may become involved at the post publication stage.

Preface

The original inspiration for this book was the overwhelming response to the original "Up Stephen's Brae" about my own experiences at Inverness Royal Academy from 1965 - 71 which sold out four separate print runs in 1995. Apart from the unexpected demand, I was extremely pleased about the positive feedback the book received and surprised at the age range of the people who had read it.

This told me that there were former pupils (and others) out there who were keen enough to read about an era other than their own but who might be even more interested in something which covered a much wider period, including when they were at school themselves. Hence the idea of 'Further Up Stephen's Brae' was born.

Clearly a different approach was required this time. I initially opted to rely principally on reproducing old magazine material with contributions from FPs through the ages as a secondary source, leaving very little original writing of my own.

From the very start I was determined that 'Further Up Stephen's Brae' would not be a rigorous history but essentially, once again, a series of anecdotal pictures of school life. However as I began to peruse the various sources available.... school magazines, log books, Robert Preece's magnificent archive etc..... it soon became apparent that a rich vein of material was available.

As a result, I began to write a lot more of the text myself, linking together the results of rather more extensive research than I had originally envisaged. But although the book took longer to produce in this altered format it is still essentially anecdotal in nature, with many of the initially intended sources still drawn upon.

An opening chapter summarises days gone by of which there will be virtually no survivors now. Chapter 2 looks at the school's contribution to the Great War which is surprisingly well documented. Thereafter the text comprises revelations of school life decade by decade until the end of the 1970s, covering personalities and incidents which many will still remember.

So whenever you were at school, even if it wasn't this one, I hope you enjoy this account of life at Inverness Royal Academy through the ages.

Charles Bannerman
Culduthel,
October 1999.

the early years

Although Inverness Royal Academy was not founded until 1792, its origins extend back to the first half of the 13th century, with compelling evidence that the school, as presently constituted, is the product of a continuous evolutionary process stretching over almost eight centuries.

Around 1233, King Alexander II founded a Priory of Black Friars in the town, situated in the area of the present Friars Street. This particular order afforded education a high priority, so with the priory there was born a Monastic School. After the battle of Largs in 1263, two of its masters were among the Scottish party which went to Norway to negotiate the handing over of the Norse Kingdom of the Isles to Scotland.

There is evidence that by 1557 at the latest this Monastic School had evolved into one of the Grammar Schools which were by now appearing across the country. In 1574 this institution moved from "The Auld Scule" on Friars Street to the site on Bank Lane which until 1990 was occupied by the Courier Office. That is why Bank Lane until the 19th Century was known as School Vennel.

Then in 1668, or very shortly thereafter, the Grammar School once again moved, this time to Dunbar's Hospital in Church Street. Among this building's famous pupils was James Wolfe who was to capture Quebec from the French in 1759. Wolfe was an ADC to the Duke of Cumberland in Inverness after the Battle of Culloden in 1746 and attended mathematics classes at the Grammar School during his stay in the town.

Inverness Royal Academy, the successor to the Grammar School, was first conceived in 1786 and has its origins in discussions about the merger of Aberdeen's then two Universities, King's and Marischal. A meeting of the "Freeholders, Commisioners of Supply, Justices of the Peace and other Gentlemen Heritors of the County of Inverness" on 21st November of that year concluded that any surplus funds resulting from the Aberdeen union should be dedicated to the foundation of an Academy in Inverness. They also concluded that such an institution should be created even if the Aberdonians were not prepared to part with their money.

Two months later, subscribers to this scheme were invited. In just over a year £2290 had been raised and by 1791 this had gone up to £4468 12s. Much of that money came from Highlanders who had gone to the West Indies to trade in tobacco and sugar. On 10th April, 1792 Mr. James Weir was appointed Rector, presiding over a curriculum which comprised Latin, Greek, French,

the early years Writing, Arithmetic, Book keeping, Mathematics, Geography, Fortification, Gunnery, History, Natural Philosophy, Chemistry and Astronomy. Fees for various classes varied from 6s per session and 1s to the Rector to £1 11s 6d per session and 2s to the Rector.

On 16th July 1792, a brand new building was opened on New Street (now Academy Street) just to the south of its junction with Strothers Lane. Inverness Academy was born. The following year, a Royal Charter was acquired at considerable expense, and the title Inverness Royal Academy came into use for the first time.

Inverness Royal Academy, 1792-1895

James Weir lasted only a year before being dismissed in 1793 for ill health - he was an epileptic. The directors did not expect him to return after one particular episode but he lived on until 1839. His successor, Dr. John M'Omie, had to be warned after he was seen very regularly about the streets of Inverness when he should have been running the affairs of the school. Another early Rector, Matthew Adam, was dismissed after a trip to London in 1839 to buy scientific apparatus became an extended holiday in the capital. And during what seems to have been a particularly scandalous early period in the school's history, there also appears to have been concern about relations between the school's female janitor and boys of the Sixth Form!

What this book is about is to give a flavour of life at Midmills over a wider period and in the eyes of rather more people than the original "Up Stephen's Brae", principally over a period which readers will remember or be able to identify with. We should therefore be prepared to move swiftly on to the school's next watershed of 1895 when the Midmills building was opened, but we can still, on our way, afford to indulge in one or two snapshots of the 19th Century on Academy Street.

maths notebook - 1830s

One legacy which is there for all to see in the present Royal Academy building at Culduthel is to be found on the boards which carry the names of the Medallists (as the duces were originally called) from 1811 onwards. At that time it was the practice to award the Medal alternately for Mathematics and Classics and a string of winners on the first board is broken only by the statement in conspicuous gold paint that: "The Mathematical Medal of 1849 was really won by but not awarded to Miss Maggie Fraser, Church St." Sexism was clearly alive and well at Inverness Royal Academy in the mid 19th century and it was over 40 years before Kate Lobban became the school's first official female dux when she took the Mathematical Medal in 1891.

The school archive contains, among much other material, log books which rectors had to keep, summarising the important day to day features of the

the early years

running of the school. These exist from 1881 onwards and are frequently revealing.

For the first year or so, the log book seems to have been not much more than a record of staff absence. This remains a strong theme in later log books, but in the early 1880s staff appear to have been obliged to sign themselves back to work with a description of the reason for absence. These mainly comprised the predictable illnesses such as congestion of the lungs, sore foot or a heavy cold. However poor Mr. Thomson had to confess in his own hand to a bout of diarrhoea.

It seems to have been a compassionate regime in these days, judging by the incidence of permitted absence due to family illness. Also, in 1898, Mr. George Easton attributed his absence on 17th and 18th January to "writing address for HRH the Duke of Edinburgh." The strain may have been too much for on February 7th, 8th and 9th he was off school again - this time with pleurisy.

However there were also self inflicted ailments and many a boy appears to have suffered sometimes quite serious injuries during frequent fights between groups from the Academy and from Dr. Bell's Institution just round the corner in Farraline Park. Sometimes it would run to no more than snowball fights with the "Bellers" but on other occasions, major conflict between large groups from the respective schools would break out.

In 1892 "The Academical" was founded and the first series appears to have run on a more or less monthly basis for around three years. Several of these magazines still survive in the School Archive and "The Academical" was to reappear briefly again around the time of World War 1. To be realistic, much of it is pretty dry and the publication is desperately short of gripping material, but the cover is of some interest. It is the creation of the Art master of the time, a Frenchman by the name of Pierre Delavault who is best known for the "Delavault Prints" - a set of small colour paintings of the town in the late 19th century.

Although this cover (shown on page 10) distorts reality in the extreme, the design does pack into one rectangle many of the major features of the Inverness skyline of the time, with the old suspension bridge particularly prominent.

February 1895 was a landmark for Inverness Royal Academy with the opening of its new building "up Stephen's Brae". Relatively simple in structure, with ground floor classrooms giving on to the hall and upper floor rooms leading out on to a gallery, these new premises were to be extended four times in less than 80 years. This was to be home for Inverness Royal Academy until 1979 and a crucial feature of many a young person's life.

> ## OPENING OF THE NEW ACADEMY.
>
> The teaching staff and pupils of the Royal Academy began work in the new buildings at Abertarff yesterday, and the workmen entered into occupation of the old school in Academy Street. The new Institution is, from an architectural point of view, a pleasant contrast to its predecessor. Its erection has entailed an expenditure by the Academy Board of £10,000; and designed by Messrs Ross & Macbeth, it has every appearance, externally and internally, of answering the many purposes of a modern educational institution. Facing Stephen's Brae, the new building stands within its own grounds, and forms a fine level stretch of about 5½ acres. The structure has a very handsome appearance, and is designed in the Elizabethan style of architecture, having two spacious flats. Entrance is by a broad flight of steps which leads into the outer hall, at the end of which a corridor runs along the breadth of the building, separating the front block from the main portion of the school. To the front there are rooms for the rector and the other teachers. The large central hall, measuring 70 by 30 feet, occupies the centre of the floor, and is excellently adapted for examinations, science classes, and entertainments. The hall is overlooked by side galleries, to which admission is gained by broad flights of stairs. On the ground floor on either side are the ordinary class-rooms. The gallery stairs give access to the science laboratory and lecture rooms on the right wing, and to the art and modelling rooms on the left wing, all on the upper floor. The rooms for the teaching of modern languages, needlework, cookery, and domestic economy, and senior and junior music, are in the front of the first floor. All these rooms are large, lofty, and well ventilated. In June 1893 the foundation stone of the new Academy was laid with full Masonic honours by the Earl of Haddington, Most Worshipful Grand Master Mason of Scotland. Another ceremony took place yesterday, by way of formally opening the School. A very large number of ladies and gentlemen, including parents and guardians of the pupils, assembled in the central hall.
>
> *Inverness Courier, 26th Feb 1895*

The Inverness Courier of 26th February 1895 gives a copious account of that opening day when the entire school marched from the old premises to the new.

Apart from the move to a new building, 1895 also saw the appointment of a new rector and the appearance of a new coat of arms. The school had not, apparently, done particularly well under George Bruce between 1888 and 1894 and emerged badly from two HMI reports of that period.

But it was transformed on the arrival of William J. Watson, who only got the job on the casting vote of the acting Chairman of Governors following interviews in public. Watson had Firsts in Classics from both Oxford and Aberdeen and was an Oxford shot putt blue into the bargain. He spent 14 successful years at Inverness Royal Academy before becoming Rector of the Royal High School in Edinburgh in 1909 and then Professor of Celtic Languages at Edinburgh University in 1914.

The coat of arms, which is still the basis of the school's extremely well known

THE ACADEMICAL.

No. 2. Vol. I.   *INVERNESS, MARCH, 1892.*   Price 2d.

CONTENTS.

The Centenary of the Academy.................. By *Ian.*
Many-Sided Chat............................. By *The Editor.*
............Our Rector (Portrait and Sketch)............
..................A Voice from Glasgow..................
St George of England........................ By *The Rector.*
.... From the Floor of the Class-room ....
Dorothy...By *Ethel.*
Experiences of an Amateur Photographer..........By *A. M.*
Our Girls...By *Toby.*
The Influenzaed Teacher.......................By *W. M. G.*
The Highlanders at Tel-el-Kebir .... By *E. R.*
.... From an Old Boy's Scrap Book ....
...................News from the Universities.................
....................The Student's Corner...................

THE CENTENARY OF THE ACADEMY.

WHAT a sleepy old town Inverness must have been one hundred years ago ! There were no railways then, no telegraph, and indeed, no good coaches. News took a long time to travel, and people did not know then, as they do now, what their fellow-beings in other places were doing. Accordingly, when any great event occurred in their midst, you may imagine what excitement there would be amongst the good folk of the burgh for that precious something to talk about. So the sixteenth of July, 1792, was a day that was awaited by the townspeople of Inverness with the greatest impatience. That day was to see the opening of the institution in which we are most interested. The long-looked for day arrived at last, and the Academy was formally opened.

A Mr Weir was the first rector, and there were about two hundred pupils, or students, as they were then called, on the roll during the first session. Some of the duties of the teachers were rather remarkable. For instance, it was the business of the Latin master to attend to the coals. The school did not at first appear to be particulary fortunate in regard to its choice of teachers, for there were continual squabbles amongst the masters themselves, and between them and the directors, and frequent changes were made in the teaching staff during the first few months. The students were also inclined to be unruly, and the directors more than once ordered the head-master to mete out severe corporal punishment to those guilty of disturbing the academic calm. We further learn that the students did not pay their fees as well as they ought. Besides their class fees, every student was required to pay 1s 6d per session for coals and candles.

Mr Weir's term of office as rector was not a lengthened one ; he was seized with severe epileptic fits, and died towards the close of the year 1839. Dr MacOmie was appointed rector in his stead. Besides other subjects the new rector had to teach natural philosophy and chemistry, thus showing that the Academy from the first was not merely an elementary school. With Dr MacOmie's appointment, all troubles did not, however, cease, for we learn that he was frequently seen on the street during class hours. However, being censured for his conduct, he thereafter devoted more attention to his school duties.

These, then, are some jottings regarding the early history of the school, but it is not my intention to go further into this subject in this article ; a historical sketch of the school will be given in a future number. I would rather here remind the reader that the centenary, the one hundredth anniversary of the opening of the school, is close upon us, and the question is, in what way can we best celebrate it? When men go to distant parts of the world there are two pictures which they are always endeavouring to recall—one is that of their old home, and the other that of their old school. And if they were to return to their native country, these are the two places which they are first to visit. The smallest thing connected with either interests them. Only the other day I received a letter from an old academical in Australia, in which he asked me if the blackboard that used to grace the Academy Hall when he was in school was there yet? If small matters such as these are of so great interest to old pupils, would they not be grieved to learn that the centenary of the Academy had come and gone unnoticed ?

the early years badge, was designed around the same time by P.J. Anderson, librarian of King's College, Aberdeen and a former pupil.

Both in the Academy Street building and in the new one, a preoccupation with attendance levels is another feature of days gone by and school managers appear to have made very regular checks of each and every register in the school. Even compared with the current age of League Tables and published HMI reports, scrutiny levels of all aspects of school life appear to have been very high indeed. In addition to the regular attendance checks, there are also more or less annual HMI reports, in stark contrast with more recent days when the next full inspection of the school following one in 1981 was in 1997.

Although in these days and for a long time to come, HMI reports would remain internal affairs not to be published, the descent of the Inspector upon the classroom was an awesome experience for staff and pupils alike. When delivered, reports were usually transcribed into the log book. In general, from W. J. Watson's time onwards, these were favourable, as the extract on page 14 from the 1913 report shows. And although this was written over 80 years ago, more than a little of its style and tone seem to have survived up to the present day in similar documents.

By this time George Morrison was well into his decade in charge between 1910 and 1920, although W. J. Watson had originally been succeeded by his namesake Gilbert Watson. However he held the post for only 15 months before embarking upon a distinguished career in the Inspectorate. He died in 1987, aged 104.

George Morrison came to Inverness from Robert Gordon's College in Aberdeen where he had been Senior Classics Master and it was to that institution that he would return as rector in 1920. He was also an accomplished musician and when he retired in 1934 he became M.P. for the Scottish Universities for eleven years.

In many instances it is very difficult to make much of the school roll and actual attendance figures, both of which appear to have been extremely variable. During the 1880s the roll, including the junior school, seems to have been in the mid 200s. The log book quite frequently records both the roll and the numbers in attendance and there are many quite considerable variations, although the general trend is upwards.

One set of figures, for instance, appear to record the total number of pupils attending the Junior and Senior (Primary and Secondary) departments during each session. This records 243 for 1888 - 89, rising to 275 in 1894 - 95 and then to 360 in 1895 - 96, the first whole session for which the new Midmills building was open. For the rest of the 19th century and into the 20th the roll seems to have been reasonably stable in the mid to low 300s before beginning a steady rise.

On the other hand, of the 334 who appear to have attended at some time during session 1899 - 1900, the average turnout is recorded as 261, or a not particularly impressive 78%. This figure is fairly consistent with others given at similar times, although disease epidemics (measles is referred to more than once) did sweep through the place, detracting from the numbers even more.

One log book entry just after the turn of the century gives a breakdown of the status of the pupils. Predictably most of them (251) paid fees but on the other hand there were also 7 Free Scholars, 7 Bursars, 12 MacKintosh Bursars and 36 County Council Free Scholars. At that time, and for a number of years to come, money was the most certain route into Inverness Royal Academy, although gifted children from poor families were reasonably well provided for.

Occasional references to the curriculum give interesting insights into what was taught and in 1899 students of French could expect to be studying Perrault's Fairy Tales while the younger years were introduced to the language through "MacKay and Curtis", apparently the favoured textbook of the day. In German it was the "Lehrbuch der Deutsche sprache" and Beresford Webb's Grammar, leading on to Goethe and Schiller.

The joys of Caesar's Invasion of Britain awaited the Latin class along with Ovid and Livy while the Grecians predictably studied the Iliad among other texts.

The world was fairly comprehensively covered in the Geography class, with an understandable emphasis on Europe and the Empire. In English it was 'The Merchant of Venice' in Class IV and 'Julius Caesar' in Class V (covered as late as the 1970s in the same sequence but two years earlier). The Sixth Form studied 'The Tempest' and there was also 'The Lady of the Lake' and MacAulay's 'Life of Johnson'.

It may seem surprising that the life of one who described a "Scotchman's" best prospect as the high road to England should be up for study at this leading light of Highland education, but the History syllabus also betrays something of a South of the Border bias.

Class VI may have studied 1707 - 1832 (Union of the Parliaments to the Reform Act) but periods before that were strictly dated in accordance with the reigns of kings - of England. In Class IV it was Henry VII to the Restoration (1485 - 1660) and in V it was 1066 - 1307, in other words William the Conqueror to Edward I (otherwise known as the Hammer of the Scots).

Junior Students.

Cookery:—

Cookery has been well taught and the results of the practical tests were very satisfactory.

Laundry Work:—

The results of the practical tests were on the whole good.

Needlework:—

Some very good Needlework was seen at this Centre and the students had on the whole done very well. That they had not all reached an equally high standard was due in a great measure to the variety in the amount of instruction they had received before they entered on the Junior Student Course here.

The Assembly Hall at the turn of the century

Sporting life seems to have been active at the Royal Academy round the turn of the century with football and cricket both flourishing, as well as girls' tennis where there were plans to form a club. In 1899 some Class III pupils complained bitterly in a letter to the Rector about older boys pinching the best football. And although up until the early 1990s Inverness Royal Academy may have been perceived very much as a "rugby school", the code of the oval ball seems to have been a relatively late arrival - possibly not until after the First World War - whereas football is of much longer standing. Also for 1899 there is a detailed inventory of cricket equipment revealing that the school owned but seven cricket balls, three of them in poor shape.

There was also more than a passing incidence of indiscipline, with truancy a recurring theme although it was an offence which attracted no mercy for those caught. On 13th September 1898 the log book records that Arthur Fraser played truant. Then in red ink beside this entry, W.J. Watson adds the note "16 lashes".

On 8th December "Peter D. MacKintosh brought to school by his sister *the early years* and confessed to having played truant. Said Miss Burns too hard on him, sending him many times to be punished by Mr. Robson for talking and not knowing the lesson. Geography and history v. hard. Wants back to the Central School."

Nowadays the first instinct of trained Guidance staff might be that this was a pupil who was completely out of his depth and in need of help. In stark contrast, more red ink records the remedy of a century ago - "8 lashes and warning."

However Mr. Watson would still have been regarded as a disciplinary liberal compared with his predecessors at the beginning of the century. The report of a committee appointed by the directors to examine the state of the school in 1834 (by which time sanctions had already become less severe) observes that: "In regard to punishments it may be remarked that corporal punishment and expulsion are, by minute of 17th December 1800, threatened by the Directors in cases of absence from Church. The precise nature of the former is not specified but it is well known that besides the minor flagellation in the several classes, a major flagellation has occasionally been resorted to in the Hall, in presence of the whole Teachers and Scholars, in cases of aggravated delinquency. An order of the Directors to this effect stands recorded 2nd February 1802 which seems to have been called forth by the excessive and intemperate castigation of one of the students in his class. The Record, however, has not been burdened with any other notice of this practice, and your committee rejoice to say that for a good many years it has not been had recourse to within this Academy. Some cases are noticed of severe and harsh treatment of the Students by the Teachers, but these are not of recent date, and at present corporal punishment, even to a limited extent, is seldom resorted to."

However any interpretation of this is bound to depend on the writer's definition of "severe and harsh treatment". One account of schooldays in the early 1870s refers to a classics master who was wont to belt out every syllable of the sentence "Dulce et decorum est pro patria mori" on the palm of any pupil who made only the most minor error in its pronunciation.

Along rather more enlightened lines, in October 1898 the Rector records: "Mrs. Johnston, Victoria Terrace, asked that her daughter (Class V) should be asked to discontinue from Geometry and Algebra. She did not understand anything of it. Examined the girl at 4pm and found a fair foundation up to and including factors and requested her to try the examination tomorrow and wait for light. See teacher."

The young Miss Johnston's difficulty may have been genuine and may indeed have persisted despite diligent study. However there was still a hard core of wasters - even in the younger years. In January 1899, A. MacKenzie (Class 1) was: "reproved for idleness and smoking cigarettes. Reproved John Bartleman (Class 1) for smoking cigarettes. JB promised to do so no more. Jo Birnie (Class 1) had smoked half cigarette. He and JB promised to tell their parents."

The same year Mr. Roddie the Music master appears to have suffered at the hands of reluctant choristers and there was something of a running battle with one H. Roberts who persistently refused to sing.

In March 1907 Lewis MacKenzie's parents in Lovat Road were informed that their offspring had been expelled for persistent truancy and in particular for frequenting ice cream parlours in Eastgate and also billiard halls. This was a school tradition which was to continue effectively unaltered for as long as the Royal Academy was situated up Stephen's Brae, although the ice cream parlours may latterly have given way to numerous town cafes such as the Washington Soda Fountain and the Cafe George.

However it was not only pupils who were capable of misbehaviour. On 22nd November 1912 the log book records that: "A serious panic was caused in Classes 4 and 5 Lower by the attempt of Mr. Blyth to enforce corporal punishment on Duncan MacPhail, Class 5. The Chairman of the School Board visited the Academy the same afternoon and the matter was reported to him."

Then on the 27th: "The Academy managers with the Board's legal adviser investigated the occurrence of Friday 22nd. At a meeting of School Board in the evening Mr. Blyth was suspended and notice to this effect was given to the Rector."

Between then and Christmas there are various references to the enquiry and how Mr. Blyth's classes were covered. Then on January 8th 1913: "At a special meeting of School Board, motion to terminate Mr. Blyth's engagement was carried. Suspension continued during the three months of notice."

Three days later the School was blessed by a much happier occasion when the new Science and Art building was opened, after several much lamented delays. This new block, running parallel with Midmills Road, comprised Science Labs (Rooms 17 to 20 by the post 1961 numbering) and a new Gym on the ground floor and upstairs several classrooms, including new Art accommodation (Rooms 23 to 30). The formal opening was performed in the gym by Mr. J. Annan Bryce M.P. although it was to be some weeks before these new facilities became fully operational. Furthermore, until the creation of the new Technical High School on Montague Row in 1934, some of this accommodation had to be shared with that institution. The fact that the timetables of these two schools did not match apparently created much chaos.

the early years

The extra space took a lot of pressure off the original 1895 building and also widened the range of curricular facilities, opening the way for a rapid increase in the roll in the years to come.

By now Inverness Royal Academy was in effect a local authority school, although still fee paying. Since its foundation it had been independently run and financed, but these finances collapsed in 1908 and it was taken over by the Burgh School Board. However they continued to look on the place as the Jewel in the Crown of education in the Highlands and left with it many of the privileges of independence such as fees and longer holidays.

But by now the storm clouds of war were beginning to descend on Europe, all over which, as Sir Edward Grey observed, the lights were going out.

the first world war

Former pupils of Inverness Royal Academy, taking their lead from the national mood of the time, were not slow to rally to the colours following Britain's entry into World War 1 on 4th August 1914. By November 1918, 491 of them had served and of these 83 made the supreme sacrifice. This was an appalling 17% in a conflict where three quarters of a million British dead represented a broadly similar overall proportion for the country as a whole.

Although disruptions on the Home Front in this conflict were not as considerable as they would be between 1939 and 1945, the war which so many had thought would be over by Christmas 1914 was soon to take a dreadful toll of the nation's youth. One in six of the FPs who left these shores lie buried on battlefields in Flanders, Gallipoli and Mesopotamia or in unmarked maritime graves.

It did not take long for the previously innocuous arrival of a telegram to acquire a whole new, sinister significance as military casualties grew amid stalemate on the Western Front. Many, many telegrams arrived in Inverness during a conflict where time and again the military would be shown, but never apparently learned, that it simply was no longer possible to walk through defences endowed with 20th century weapons technology, despite saturation artillery bombardment.

We have two war service numbers and a memorial issue of "The Inverness Academical" to thank for a very detailed picture of the school's contribution to World War 1, both at home and at the Front. Publication of regular issues of the magazine was suspended on the outbreak of hostilities and it was June 1916 before a reasonably accurate Roll of Honour could be compiled to allow the production of the first war service number to go ahead.

In June 1917 a second, similar, updated publication appeared which gives further details of the efforts and sacrifices of Old Boys. The passage (overleaf) from it is something of a paradox. On the one hand it appears to applaud the high proportion of FPs who had aspired to "Officer" ranks while at the same time it deplores the class system which dominated the Army.

It was also conceded from the start that recognition should be given to what Old Girls had done in the field of military medicine but the second publication was forced to reveal that progress in this respect had been slow. It admits that "we can only record the fact that the evidence already in our possession shows that our Old Girls are playing a great and noble part in the present war".

OUR WAR RECORD.

Our list of Old Boys who are serving, or who have served, with the colours in the present war is still very incomplete, but already it contains 404 names, a truly remarkable record for a school of the size of the Academy, which for the last 30 years has seldom had more, and very frequently has had less, than 150 boys on its register in any one year. This means that nearly three times the average number of boys attending the Academy yearly are already known to have served in the present war; and, though comparisons are unpleasant things, we may be pardoned if we remark that this is a record which few schools in the country can equal.

In our last number we observed that until the middle of last century the Academy was a veritable cradle of soldiers, but during the long years of peace which succeeded the Mutiny the Army became a resort more for men of means than for poorer men of warlike spirit who wished to follow a military career, and that in consequence, during the last forty years of the 19th century, the Old Boys who took up the profession of arms were comparatively few in number. This makes our record in the present war all the more creditable. When war broke out only 10 of our Old Boys held commissions in the Navy and Army, and even if we add Territorials the total is only 21. To-day the number of Old Boys whose names appear on our Roll as officers in His Majesty's Forces is 179, and of these 16 have already laid down their lives for their country. These figures are both a tribute to the quality of the men whom the Highlands and the Academy produce, and a condemnation of the military system which makes it impossible for such men to hold the King's Commission in time of peace.

Analysis of the lists of casualties and FPs on active service, which hold a prominent place in all three magazines, is revealing although by 1917 details are restricted by wartime censorship, with only the regiment and not the battalion published.

The first FP to die in the war was Private Albert Corner of the 4th Camerons at Neuve Chapelle on March 11th 1915. Ironically he was the son of a local bank actuary and a German mother, Hedwig Corner. Albert's brother Otto was killed less than four months later while another brother Harold was severely wounded. In an era of very large families, no fewer than seven Corner brothers served their country between this and the Boer War.

In a conflict where many families suffered multiple tragedies there were also the MacKintoshes of 12, Charles St. who lost two sons in just six weeks in the spring of 1916. Dr. John MacKintosh returned from South Africa to serve. Both he and his brother Donald appear to have been involved in the Dardanelles campaign and both died in hospital in Egypt, the rear base for that enterprise.

Round the corner there were ex-Bailie and Mrs. Maclean of 28, Hill Terrace, five of whose sons served. One of them, Lance Corporal William MacLean, was wounded at Ypres in April 1915 and died in hospital at Woolwich just over a fortnight later while Private Alex. was killed at Loos that September. Another brother, Norman, who was promoted from the ranks to Lieutenant for services in the field, was severely wounded.

In addition to the five MacLean brothers there were also four sons of the former music master Ernest Kesting who himself died in July 1916 at the age of 86. Three of them were on active service while a fourth, the Rev. August Kesting, was Officiating Clergyman to British troops in Paris. But in war, death never distributes itself evenly. All four Kesting brothers survived.

Perhaps the greatest sacrifice was made by parents who gave all they had. In St. Andrews Cathedral there is a memorial tablet which reads: "In loving memory of James Donald Davidson, Private, 4th Cameron Highlanders (T), the only son of his parents Donald and Emily Davidson. He answered his country's call at the beginning of the Great War and fell in action at Festubert, France on the 18th of May 1915, in the 26th year of his age."

The delay of the first fatality until March 1915 is consistent with the observation made in the second "Academical" that few FPs were members of the Regular Army which bore the brunt of the fighting on the battlefields of Mons, Le Cateau, the Marne and in particular the First Battle of Ypres in the early months of the war. On the other hand the volunteers, Territorials and the New Army who flooded into France in 1915 contained a much larger Royal Academy contingent. Correspondingly, the Roll of Honour shows that 22 of the 38 deaths up to mid 1917 took place between April and September 1915. The first crop of volunteers must have suffered heavily.

At least the 1916 edition of "The Academical" gives details down to the battalion in which men served and the frequency with which the 4th Battalion of the Cameron Highlanders appears gives an interesting insight. When Britain began to improvise a mass, volunteer army towards the end of 1914, it was organised so that additional battalions supplemented the two established Regular Army formations of each of the existing regiments.

As a result, the 4th Camerons, a Territorial unit set up just before the war, *the first world war* was one of the earlier battalions raised from the Inverness area, attracting many of the first volunteers. This unit, which went out to France in February 1915 and into action the following month, is by far the most frequently referred to in the list of FPs on active service and it suffered horrific casualties.

No fewer than 53 FPs are named as having served in it up to June 1916. These were men who were educated together, volunteered together, served and lived together on the Western Front..... and many also died together. Nine of the 22 FPs who died during 1915 were with the 4th Camerons. These included its 51 year old Commanding Officer Lt. Col. Alex. Fraser who was also a Town Councillor and Magistrate. But as far as Inverness was concerned this would merely have been the tip of the iceberg. In this battalion there would have been many, many more local men who met their fate together on the killing fields of Flanders during 1915 and later - and this was just one of many battalions.

The resulting stream of fateful telegrams arriving in the town that summer would be repeated many times over the length and breadth of the land before the end of 1918. In a war where battalions drawn from very specific areas were sent into action wholesale into a hail of machine gun bullets and shrapnel in huge offensives, a home town could find itself devastated in the course of a day or two as the telegrams began to arrive in their dozens.

In an extreme case, 585 "Accrington Pals" were killed or wounded on the same day on the Somme in 1916. Inverness would have been no exception and in Dingwall one war memorial bears the names of 41 local men who died at Cambrai in a two day period in 1917.

Typical of the manner in which men were sent "over the top" in their thousands in this conflict are three concentrations of deaths during 1915 on the school's Roll of Honour. These were on and around April 23rd at Ypres, May 18th at Festubert (in an action where the 4th Camerons bore particularly heavy casualties) and September 25th at Loos where five Royal Academy FPs were killed or mortally wounded on the same day.

Perhaps the best known of those killed at Loos, in this case at Hill 70, was Major James Barron of the family which until the late 1980s owned the Inverness Courier. Barron, who had been an outstanding student of British History, Political Economy and English Literature at Edinburgh University, was wounded in action on September 25th with the 7th Camerons and died in a German Field Hospital two days later.

This meant that the business, which for decades also printed Royal Academy magazines and "Academicals", passed to his brother Dr. Evan Barron who

The Late Major JAMES BARRON

was a leading light in the Old Boys' Club. Also an eminent writer and historian, Dr. Barron edited the Courier until he handed over in the 60s to his niece, James's daughter Eveline Barron who had never known her father. For many years there hung behind the public counter in the old Courier Office in Bank Lane an artist's impression of the Battle of Loos where James Barron met his death.

Hill 70, the site of James Barron's death, did not leave as indelible a mark on the town of Inverness as its neighbour Hill 60 near Ypres. The 1st and 2nd Camerons were heavily engaged there during the Second Battle of Ypres with enormous casualties. As a result, this geographical feature became synonymous in Inverness with fighting to the extent that I remember my grandmother, who was a teenager in Inverness during the war, referring to one particularly rough tenement block off Grant Street as "Hill 60".

The Courier gave extensive coverage to the wartime activities of the 4th Camerons, who in their first three months in France suffered no fewer than 413 casualties. One of a mass of eye witness accounts of their action at Festubert is given by an unnamed contributor, who may or may not have been an FP and who described the horror of the scene most vividly.

"No sooner did we make our appearance in the open than a hot fire from rifles and machine guns opened on us, and officers and men began to fall. Captain Ronald Macdonald was hit straight away and so was Lieutenant Thompson. But we soon discovered that the enemy's fire was not the only danger we had to face. We had gone forward only a few yards when we were up against a deep ditch full of filthy water which none but the strongest and most agile could jump, weighed down as we were with arms and equipment. And it was now pitch dark and rain was falling heavily. The majority of the men failing to clear the ditch disappeared up to the neck in the slimy water and it was with

the first world war

much difficulty that they were pulled on to the opposit[e] bank by their stronger comrades. In the course of th[e] advance, two such ditches and several slightly les[s] formidable had to be negotiated."

More than 80 years on, it is difficult to conceive of how men many of them intelligent and well educated, could, at the blow of whistle, stand up and walk into such murderous fire, bogged down b[y] such impossible terrain. It is equally difficult to conceive of the mentalit[y] of the senior officers who issued such orders - again and again.

The death penalty for disobedience was doubtless a great incentive to g[o] over the top. It is also very easy to use present day values in assessing somethin[g] which took place a long time ago under completely different social condition[s]. Furthermore this was an era when it was considered noble to "die for King an[d] Empire" (in hundreds of thousands). Many FPs returned home from the end[s] of the earth to do just that, even although, unlike during World War 2, ther[e] was no real direct threat either to King or Empire. Having had "dulce et decorur[m] est pro patria mori" literally belted into them at Inverness Royal Academ[y] may or may not have had an additional effect on some.

In contrast with these earlier actions of 1915, of the 19,000 deaths from horrific 57,000 British casualties on the first day of the Battle of the Somm[e] on 1st July 1916, only two are FPs. One was a Royal Engineer, the other Royal Scot and the statistic probably reflects the units which happened to b[e] unlucky enough to be sent in on that fateful day.

Records reveal that FPs served in units as diverse as the Calcutta Scottis[h] the Royal Naval Transport Service, the Canadian Infantry and the Nyasalan[d] Expeditionary Force. But by far the biggest representations are in the Highlan[d] regiments, particularly the Seaforths and Camerons which are those most loca[l] to Inverness. From these two regiments, only the 1st Camerons were selecte[d] for action on July 1st 1916. This battalion, which suffered 394 casualties from around 1000 men on that single day, must have been largely devoid of FP[s] otherwise entries in "The Academical" would have been several. Old Boy[s] did, however, clearly take part in later weeks of the battle.

One of the July 1st deaths was that of Pte. Hugh W. Melven of the Roya[l] Scots who became the second member of his family to perish in just over [a] year. His brother, a Cameron Highlander although not apparently an FP, wa[s] another of the many local casualties at Festubert in May 1915. It was the Melve[n] family which for many years ran the bookshop which traded under that nam[e] in Union Street before it was taken over by James Thin.

Many obituaries appear in both the 1916 and 1917 "Academicals" - strictl[y] "in order of rank, and as far as possible, seniority. Where the seniority is doubtful, the notices are arranged according to date of death." The following are just two entries from this obsessively hierarchical list.

The Late Pte. HUGH W. MELVEN.
1st July 1916.

It is with no ordinary regret, says the "Inverness Courier" of 11th July 1916, that we announce to-day the death in action, on 1st July, at the Battle of the Somme, of Pte. Hugh W. Melven, Royal Scots, youngest son of the late Bailie Joseph Melven, bookseller, Inverness, and Mrs Melven, Hay Lodge, Nairn. A little over a year ago Pte. Melven's eldest brother, Lance-Corpl. D. C. Melven, 4th Cameron Highlanders, was killed in action at Festubert, and very great sympathy is felt for the mother and sisters now doubly bereaved.

Pte. Hugh Melven was educated at the Academy, and on leaving school joined his brother in the well-known business which the latter conducted in Union Street. He subsequently went to Edinburgh to gain further experience, and there the outbreak of war found him. Pte. Melven at once enlisted in one of the Service Battalions of the Royal Scots, and with it proceeded to France. He was home on leave only three weeks ago, and rejoined his Battalion at the front a day or two before the great battle north of the Somme in which he fell.

The Late Pte. GEORGE M. WATSON.
10th September 1916.

Pte. George Munro Watson, second son of Dr W. J. Watson, for many years Rector of the Academy, and now Professor of Celtic Language and Literature at Edinburgh University, was killed instantaneously by a sniper on the afternoon of 10th September 1916. His officer says in a letter that he was the keenest of soldiers, and much regretted by all who knew him. Pte. Watson would not have been 18 till last December, but his sense of patriotism was very strong, and in June 1915 he joined the Argyll and Sutherland Highlanders at the age of 16. Thereafter he joined the Royal Liverpool Rifles, and went to France in the middle of July last year. For a few weeks prior to his death he was on duty with a Tunnelling Company of the Royal Engineers. He was educated at the Academy and the Royal High School of Edinburgh.

The full list of 83 fatal casualties is published in the War Memorial number of "The Academical" which did not appear until 1921. By this time the War Memorial tablet itself, which contains the names of all who served and died,

the first world war

had been placed on the main stairs in the Midmills building. It now has pride of place outside the Lecture Theatre in the current premises at Culduthel, with the list from World War 2 beside it. To this day the School Captains continue the tradition of laying a poppy wreath there on the Friday before Armistice Sunday and also attend the Sunday parade to the town's main war memorial at Cavell Gardens.

The final list of Great War dead in the 1921 "Academical", although complete, does not give personal details such as address and regiment as in 1916 and to a lesser extent 1917. As a result our picture of the casualties and those who served in the last year and a half of the conflict is even more sketchy, but there are 45 names on the final list of dead which are additional to the 38 as at June 1917. Information at that intermediate stage would definitely have been incomplete, with extra names referring to the earlier period added later. But it is still certain that many FPs died in the last 18 months of the war, which included the Battle of Passchendaele and the "backs to the wall" opposition to the great German offensive of March and April 1918.

Brigadier-General R. A. CARRUTHERS, C.B., C.M.G

In terms of distribution of the casualties by rank, historians have observed that the loss rate among junior officers in World War 1 was three times that of the lower ranks. In the case of Inverness Royal Academy, evidence supporting this is inconclusive. Remembering that junior officers would have been vastly outnumbered by privates and NCOs, the fact that 29 of the Royal Academy FP dead - just over a third of the total - were Second Lieutenants, Lieutenants and Captains may at first sight appear to be consistent with the observation.

On the other hand a middle class, academic institution would be expected to contribute a large share of officers and just over a third of all FP recruits - survivors as well - are listed as being from these same three ranks. It is very possible that this picture may depend on other, much more complex factors, perhaps including the fact that a surprising proportion of those who survived served with the Royal Army Medical Corps where the risks may have been lower.

The War Numbers of "The Academical" also detail the many honours won by Old Boys. One of two C.M.Gs. went to Col. (Temp. Brigadier General) Robert A. Carruthers C.B. who was probably the most senior and distinguished of the FPs who served during the First World War. Born in 1862 and a member of the family which originally owned the Inverness Courier, Carruthers was educated both at the Academy and Fettes College. He was a fine sportsman and became the inaugural Scottish AAA hurdles champion in 1883.

One of the few FPs to become regular soldiers at this time, Carruthers joined the Army in the year of his athletic triumph and retired with the rank of Colonel just before the outbreak of war. He soon rejoined and was later promoted to Temporary Brigadier General on attachment to the ANZACs as Deputy Adjutant and Quartermaster General in Egypt and later at Gallipoli, before moving to France with the 1st ANZAC Corps.

One source of what must almost be the final tally of war honours is a letter of June 1918 from Evan Barron to various Old Boys launching the War Memorial Fund. It says: "Three Old Boys have been awarded the CMG, one the CB, one the CIE, five the DSO, thirteen the Military Cross, one the DCM, one the DSM, one the Military Medal and one the Croix de Guerre while 20 have been Mentioned in Despatches, several more than once."

Although the list of Old Girls on War Service never materialised, the 1916 "Academical" does contain the graphic account overleaf, of the bravery of two of them in Serbia. It was here, in the Balkans, that the war had its immediate origins following the assassination of Archduke Franz Ferdinand in June 1914 and the horrors were no less than on the Western Front.

At home, education continued relatively undisrupted at the top of Stephen's Brae, as the following excerpt (overleaf) from the school log of June 1916 shows. Apart from classes continuing uninterrupted, the usual cultural activities such as piano recitals and the well established Ettles Lecture also went on unabated. On the other hand there are also frequent references to efforts made to ease the lot of the troops at the front.

Only five staff are listed as having fought in the war although with a roll of

> **119**
>
> June
> 6 — J.S. teaching in Central P.S. Col. Forsyth and Monsignor Macqueen, managers, visited.
> 7 — After prayers the Rector made reference to the death of Lord Kitchener.
> 12 — Mr M. Morrison conducted oral exam in Hr French; saw also 2 Lower
> 13 — Mr B. Hamilton, " " Hr Maths.
> 21 — Domestic Science Exam.
> 27 — Fête, with sale of cakes, candy, fruit & flowers, opened by Mrs Fraser Mackenzie of Allangrange. This was a joint fête in behalf of Camerons Comforts Fund & Academy War Fund. Drawings & Subscriptions amounted to nearly £75.
> 28 — Distribution of Prizes & Certificates in Academy Hall. Prizes were distributed by James Barron Esq, Raverig, who presented several valuable book prizes.
>
> 23 Full Leaving Certifs., 38 Intermediate

Excerpt from school log book of 1916

under 500 and a number of female teachers, there may not have been all that many men of military age. Of the five, one - Pioneer A.T. Adam B.Sc. - lost his life while Mr. J. Anderson Robertson, Principal Teacher of English, enlisted in the summer of 1917 but was discharged less than a year later on medical grounds.

Charles Mitchell temporarily left the maths department after only a year to serve in the Camerons for almost four, reaching the rank of Captain and winning the Military Cross. He returned after the war to become Principal Teacher in 1920. But like so many veterans, he was very reluctant indeed to talk about his experiences in the trenches, although he was moved to blazing indignation by any flippant reference to the war or to its casualties.

War Service Number.

Academy Old Girls in Serbia

Among the band of heroic Scottish ladies who won so much honour as Doctors and Nurses in Serbia during the terrible ordeal of the Austrian invasion and the Serbian retreat last year were two old Academy girls, Dr Laila Muncaster and Mrs Green, the latter better known in Inverness as Miss Mary Gowenlock, a daughter of the late Mr Wm. Gowenlock of the Highland Railway.

DR MUNCASTER'S EXPERIENCES.

Dr Muncaster, who only left the Academy for Edinburgh University a few years ago, has sent the following account of her experiences to a friend in Inverness:—

You were anxious to hear something of my adventures in the Balkans. Of course it would fill a book if I were to tell you all that happened to us, so I can only give you the merest outline. I was attached to Mrs St Clair Stobart's unit, and went out to Serbia in the beginning of August. At first I did dispensary work in a country district, and treated all kinds of cases just as they came, but after the German and Bulgarian invasions started I was recalled to work in the military hospital—first at Kragujevatz and afterwards at Lapovo—a railway junction. The German aeroplanes used to come over almost daily and drop bombs on us, but beyond scaring people they did very little damage.

At last, on October 24th, we were told by the military authorities that we must clear out with our patients, as the Germans were only 15 miles away. We knew they were pretty near, as we could actually hear the whistle of the shells. We packed up all our stores, and got the patients on to a hospital train, and took them to Nish. We weren't allowed to leave the train ourselves, but were sent back to a place called Krolieve, and "dumped" there. The town was packed full of refugees, but we managed to get a big tent to live in—there were about 14 or 15 of us. From that time we became refugees ourselves, and just wandered from place to place, always hoping that the enemy would be checked, and that we could stay somewhere and get some work to do.

At last it became apparent that the whole country was being over-run, that the food was giving out, and that no good could be done by staying. We first tried to make for Monastir, and so get down to Salonika, but found at Prizend that the way was blocked by Bulgarians. We then turned north again to Ipec, in Montenegro. We walked practically all the way, and our luggage was carried by bullock carts. We encountered all kinds of weather, good and bad, but mostly bad, and slept in many queer, uncomfortable places. At Ipec our stuff was put on to pack ponies and donkeys, and we started over the mountains in detachments on foot. The road was merely a track hewn out of the hill-side. It was covered with snow and ice, and we passed hundreds of dead and dying horses, donkeys and even men. The cold was excessive, but the lack of food was the worst thing. The Serbian Army were retreating over this road with hundreds of Austrian and Bulgarian prisoners, and their sufferings were simply heartrending to behold. Poor souls! They were a brave and uncomplaining crowd, and behaved marvellously well. I never heard a sign of a quarrel or saw a drunk man among them, which says a good deal for them, I think.

We were about ten days in Montenegro, sleeping outside or in stables or in peasants' houses—just where we could. We had very little food, and couldn't buy any. We lived mostly on bovril and tea and cocoa. Finally, we got down to Scutari, in Albania, and from there down to the coast, to San Giovanni di Medua. After five days there, living under the most miserable conditions possible to imagine, an Italian ship with food for the Serbs came in, and took us over to Brindisi. From there we came straight home through Italy, Switzerland, France, and crossed over to Southampton from Havre. We were all thoroughly glad to catch sight of home again, I can tell you. We arrived on December 22nd, exactly two months after we started to trek. By the end of the journey most of us had lost nearly everything we had. We were the dirtiest and most disreputable crew imaginable. I arrived in Paris without a hat or gloves, but managed to buy them there, and to get a bath—after not having one for two months!

MRS GREEN'S ADVENTURES.

Mrs Green formed one of a party of 18 who walked all the way through the Albanian mountains, from Meladenovatz to San Giovanni de Medua. They left Meladenovatz about the beginning of October, having to evacuate the hospital there, after it had been bombed by German aeroplanes. Their journey through Albania was a terribly trying one. The winter had set in, and the roads in places were almost impassable on account of deep snow and ice. Food was very scarce, and, for over two months, doctors and nurses alike had to be contented with what nightly rest they could obtain from a little hay laid on floors of stables, cowsheds, cholera hospitals, or any other available buildings. The nursing party retreated along with the Army, and, wherever possible, they opened dressing stations in which the wounded soldiers could be attended to. The hardy and heroic qualities of the young Scotswomen were equal to the tremendous test of the journey, and they were warmly welcomed home again.

Pupils' Work for Sailors and Soldiers.

In our last number we published a statement showing that during the first twenty months of the war the pupils of the Academy, especially the girls, under the direction of Miss Middleton, had been assiduous in providing comforts for sailors and soldiers, large numbers of articles having been made and despatched to various destinations for use at the front. During the past year this excellent work has been continued, no fewer than 782 articles having been distributed among various battalions of the Cameron Highlanders, the Camerons' Christmas Fair, Mine-Sweepers, Hospitals, Queen Mary's Shower Day, and last but not least, Old Academy Boys on active service. The articles comprised socks, seamen's stockings, scarves, cuffs, cardigans, face-cloths, handkerchiefs, cigarettes, etc., etc. These were all packed and despatched free of charge by Mr David Forbes, High Street, Inverness.

Amount Collected to pay for Material.

Sessions 1914-15 and 1915-16, already acknowledged, £62 13s 11d; prize money voted by pupils—1915, £11; 1916, £12; 1917, £12; Mrs Fraser-Mackenzie of Allangrange, £4 10s; Old Academy Girls' Club, £1 10s; subscriptions received at Cake and Candy Sale, £1 19s 6d; Miss Isabella Robertson, 7s 6d; Proceeds of Pianoforte Recital, £1 10s 6d; Share of Proceeds of Fete held June 1916, £24 18s 3d; Mrs W. J. Watson, Edinburgh, 5s; Miss Barron, Ravelrig, £1; Mrs Morrison, Frithview, 3s; Mr Crampton-Smith, Royal Academy, 2s 6d; Mr Robson, do., 2s; Mr Lowson, do., 4s; Mrs Straw, 1 Victoria Terrace, 2s; Miss Margaret Stewart, 1s; Miss Smith, Royal Academy, 2s; from Six Little Girls, Royal Academy, 7s; Mrs Macrae, Cameron Barracks, 4s; Anonymous, 3s 6d; War Tea and Sale, June 1917, £16 4s 7d; total, £151 10s 3d.

Received in addition:—Mrs Howe, Castle Heather, 4 pairs socks; Miss Burns, Union Road, 8 cuts wool; Mrs Campbell, Dalcrag, 6 pairs socks; Mrs Gray, Crombagh, wool for 2 scarves. Also, numerous Cakes of Soap, Cigarettes, Handkerchiefs, etc., enclosed in socks by the pupils. 1122 eggs were also collected by the pupils during the session for the National Egg Collection.

Pupils and staff at the school certainly made their contribution to the war effort in common with so many others at the time by providing comforts for the troops. This is warmly acknowledged in both War numbers, although rather more briefly in the 1917 publication.

the first world war

It is not only this acknowledgement which has had to be curtailed in the 1917 "Academical" which runs to 56 small pages of text only, without the high quality photographs of its predecessor. The explanation comes at the very bottom of the last page where there is the comment: "We regret that owing to the great scarcity of paper, the high price of printing material of all kinds and the shortage of labour, it is not possible to issue this number at the price of less than One Shilling."

By 1917 standards this was a huge amount of money, but both magazines sold extensively and were widely distributed to the Front where many an Old Boy must have been delighted to receive at least something which was part of "home", tragic though much of its content may have been.

Then in the autumn of 1918, with revolution in the air, Germany quite suddenly collapsed and by 1919 the troops - those who had survived - were home again from the front. Inverness Royal Academy could look forward to peacetime education, a new decade and a new rector in what politicians claimed would be a "land fit for heroes".

the 1920s

In 1920 George Morrison moved on to Aberdeen and was replaced by W. Crampton Smith who had become Second Master in 1915. A man of deep religious convictions and an elder of the Crown Church across the road, Crampton Smith remained until January 1944 and is probably the earliest Rector to be remembered, at the time of writing in 1999, by any more than a tiny handful of the oldest FPs. "Crampie" was not renowned for his ability to relate to people, nor for any great capacity to inspire his pupils. However he appears to have run the school efficiently enough.

The War and its after effects still weighed heavily on the national psyche, and would do so for a long time despite the fact that this decade of Flappers and the Charleston would be dubbed the "Roaring Twenties". However the fighting had been over for more than three years before the War Memorial Number of "The Academical" finally appeared in December 1921. The publishers presumably waited until considerable efforts to mark the school's contribution to the conflict had come to fruition.

By this time fees had been abolished in the fourth and later years of the secondary department under the 1918 Education Act and the former Inverness College had been purchased and converted into a War Memorial Hostel for out of town pupils. In addition, "three acres, two roods twenty seven poles or thereby" of adjoining land was set aside for a school playing field. The College building is what, during the 1930s, became "County Buildings" on the junction of Glenurquhart Road and Ardross Street. Then in 1975 it became the Headquarters of Highland Regional Council, with an extension built rearwards into the former playing field.

The acquisition of these properties, valued at the end of the war at £5000, had been a stroke of genuis. A War Memorial Fund had been very generously subscribed to the extent of £1283 while, among other functions, a Victory Fair had raised the phenomenal sum by 1919 standards of £1040. The Trustees were still well short of their £5000, but astutely persuaded the Inverness Education Authority that the College premises were such an acquisition that it was worth their contributing £1000 to secure them. Much of the balance was made up by persuading 48 shareholders of the former College to donate 1190 shares in the premises.

A 14 ft by 6 ft War Memorial tablet, with the names of those who served painted and those who died carved on its surface, had also been provided from this fund at a cost of £300. That was unveiled in the school on the stairs at the rear of the hall, which became the library in 1961. The ceremony was performed by Viscount Finlay at noon on October 10th 1921 in the presence of a large gathering of dignatories, past and present pupils and friends. It was followed by similar proceedings at the hostel later that afternoon.

One of the very first residents of the Ardross Street hostel was a second year pupil from Tomatin named Robin MacPhee. She later became Mrs. Robert Denoon and in her old age recounted on tape to her daughter Deirdre some of her recollections of being an Inverness Royal Academy pupil in the 1920s. Deirdre Denoon, later Mrs. MacLennan, joined the school's History Deptatment in 1977 and kindly made this tape available.

North-West Corner of Hostel Quadrangle

In an extensive interview, both Mr. and Mrs. Denoon relate their memories of Inverness and Glen Urquhart from before World War 1 through to the 1920s, and this includes Mrs. Denoon's vivid memories of school and hostel life at the time.

It was suggested to her by her headmaster at Tomatin school that she should apply for a bursary at the Royal Academy, but at the time the 18 mile trip into Inverness was not one which could be performed daily and residence in the town would be a necessity. Even for some living quite close to major academic institutions at that time, the price of the eduaction which they could provide was to be uprooted from a family home at the age of twelve.

The following are Robin Denoon's recollections of school life between 1920 and 1926.

the 1920s

"I was told to go to the education headquarters at 11, High Street in Inverness on a certain day and I was put into a room with one or two other pupils from different places and given exam papers - one in arithmetic and the other was a selection of titles for composition. Later I was told I had passed my examination and I was getting £25 a year of a bursary for Inverness Royal Academy.

In those days you had to find your own accommodation and there wasn't a hostel when I went for the first year. It was during my second year that a hostel was opened for girls. Before that I stayed with my aunt at Newton of Petty near Allanfearn and I travelled in each day from Allanfearn Station. Such a lot of people travelled on that little train, for a matter of five or six miles, which was quite exciting for me.

Quite a number of pupils came from farther east, from Dalcross and the Gollanfield area, and I thought the school was marvellous - Inverness Academy up at the top of this hill, Stephen's Brae, which we had to climb. My mother went with me to school the first day and she didn't know any more about it than I did. But she took me up to the front door of the Academy. There was standing the Head Janitor in full regalia and my mother didn't know who he was. She may have thought he was the schoolmaster! He directed her to the rector's room and I was taken care of and was sent to the first classroom. It was Latin with Mr. Robson, Room 11, and I thought he was the funniest, most amusing teacher I ever saw in my life and that memory still remains. I was put into one of the front seats. I had had a little Latin from my previous schoolmaster in Tomatin, strange to say. He gave me Latin and some Algebra and French and Geometry before I went to Inverness Royal Academy so I knew the basics in Latin. I knew 'amo, amas, amat' and the First Declension and things like that. Mr. Robson was amazed at this because the other pupils in the class had come straight from Primary and didn't know anything about it at all."

Robin Denoon also has fond memories of the new hostel where she stayed for her second and subsequent years and from which she walked each morning to the top of Stephen's Brae. That was a walk which was also very different in the 1920s.

Tomnahurich Street had but a single shop while the river was spanned by the old suspension bridge. That was to be condemned as unsafe just before World War II, but it allowed tanks to pass in complete safety for six years and was not replaced until the 1960s. The bridge was incredibly narrow by modern standards and so was Bridge Street which until the early 60s contained many old buildings of character before they were replaced by their much criticised successors. Then there was High Street and before the ascent of Stephen's Brae, Eastgate which was a vehicular thoroughfare, full of tiny old shops, pubs and even a dairy. This was a walk from hostel to school with which the youngster from Tomatin was to become much more familiar over the next five years.

"It was an ideal place for a hostel becuse it was a boys' college before and the rooms were all there, the dormitories that the boys had. It was a Young Gentlemen's College before the First World War and I was among the first lot of children who went into that place. It was opened as the Inverness Royal Academy War Memorial Hostel and I remember the ceremony quite well. It was a wonderful building to me and other pupils like me because in those days we used to read those Angela Brazil story books about girls' boarding schools and here we were in these very surroundings and in the dormitories we could visualise all the things we had been reading about. We had several matrons and a nurse looking after us. There were 61 girls there and many came from places which are now regarded as quite close to Inverness but in those days there was no transport. There were people from Beauly and Drumnadrochit and Tomatin and Daviot and Carrbridge and we had many girls from the islands - from Skye and even from the Outer Hebrides where there was quite a group of Gaelic speaking girls. They were strange to us because many of us had never come in contact with Gaelic before and that sounds very strange, living in the Highlands. They were strange to us because they spoke their language among themselves. Some of them were very homesick and some of them were very, very clever and they had no difficulty with languages. Many of us became very friendly with the girls from the west."

In a further conversation with her daughter, which is reproduced in the school's 1992 Bicentenary Folio, Mrs. Denoon had other memories of her time at the hostel.

"The first dormitory I was in when I went to the hostel consisted of eight beds with enough space in between for a person to get up and dressed. Each bed had a chest of drawers and a chair beside it. There was a great big wardrobe at the end. Clothes had to be hung in it and nothing had to be lying on the floor.

We lived in a world of bells. A bell wakened you and at the next bell you had to be up with your bed stripped. We all wore gym suits, black stockings and black shoes and in summer, white panama hats with blue and gold ribbons on them. After breakfast on cold mornings the assistant matrons would make sure that everyone was wrapped up warmly and see us safely on our way to school, two by two or in a group.

After our evening meal we spent so many hours studying until bed time. The big study was at the right hand side at the front for younger girls and the small study was for classes V and VI. We all had lockers on the wall for our

the 1920s

books and sat two to a table. Lessons got first priority. We had to sit very quietly with Matron or Assistant Matron seeing that order was kept, otherwise there might be fighting or quarrelling.

At bed time every night I remember that the Matron came along to see that everything was tidy and our clothes folded on the chairs beside our beds.

'Good night, girls.'

'Good night, Miss Paterson.'

When I was older I was in a cubicle and then in my last year we were allowed to go into a bedroom with three other girls."

At the same time, boys from out of town were accommodated in a house run by Mr. Robson in Muirfield Road before arrangements were eventually made for them at Drummond Park.

Class VI.A - 1926
Roddy Campbell - 3rd from right, back row
Robin MacPhee - seated far right, front row

Mrs. Denoon takes some pride from the proportion of pupils from her class - the VIA of 1926 - who went to University, and in particular the number of girls who did so. She also remembers one "brilliant boy" to whom she refers as "Dr. Campbell" who must be the Roderick Campbell who became the dux in that year and was one of a number of gifted sons of the Balloch schoolmaster.

From the same period, Archie Dobbie, joint dux in 1929, remembers the legendary Inverness strong man Donald Dallas who taught Gym at various local schools, including the Academy, dressed in Harris tweed plus fours. And when Dallas was not teaching he could usually be found climbing mountains, breaking heavyweight records at Highland Games or acting on the stage. Donald Dallas continued to teach at the Academy until October 1935 when he was knocked over by a car in Inglis Street and appears at that point to have been invalided out of the profession.

Archie's sister Daisy remembers how the assembly hall was transformed by the Art Department into a bright backdrop for the school dance. In that respect nothing has changed in 70 years, apart from the fact that it is Jake Johnston's successors who have supervised the work in recent times. She also remembers the rare occasions when they faced not the Rector's office as for prayers but the stairs when they all gathered for the school concert or some other stage production which was acted out on the landing.

Cast of "Gods of the Mountain" - 1927

By the early 1920s the school roll had risen to over 500 and the upward trend was set to continue. This led to a further expansion of the premises

the 1920s in 1926 when a dedicated wing was opened for the Primary Department, that empire over which the legendary Kate Kennedy and her successor Alice Grant ruled for so many years. This wing runs parallel with the 1913 extension, but emanates from the opposite rear corner of the original 1895 building. As a result, three sides of what, with the next extension in 1961, became the "Quad", now existed. This latest extension allowed a further increase in pupil numbers and in September 1927 the roll is recorded as 201 in the Primary Department and 550 in the Secondary.

His Majesty's Inspectors appear to have taken a generally favourable view of the school during the 20s, with one conspicuous exception which would continue to cause them concern into the next decade. In 1927 they were as appreciative of the Primary Department ("The tone of the school throughout is all that can be desired") as they were damning of Latin.

It was ironic that the Classics inspector should have been former rector Gilbert Watson who remarked, swingeingly, that: "The efficiency of the Latin classes has been regrettably low for some time: in the past session no improvement has taken place. The results of the Leaving Certificate examination indicate in a rough way how unsuccessful the instruction has been, and a scrutiny of the individual marks reveals how poor was the work even of those who passed. The estimates of proficiency submitted by the school were far from reliable. Thorough reorganisation of the instruction is necessary, as well as more cordial co-operation among the members of the staff."

There does seem to have been light at the end of the tunnel because in 1929 he remarks: "The recent strengthening of the classical staff by the introduction of capable lady teachers should make it possible to secure a considerably higher standard in the department as a whole, but the full effect of their work is not yet evident."

However the view of his colleague Mr. MacDonald, who inspected English in 1927, may have been rather more pragmatic in a school to which entry was still principally governed by the ability to pay rather than to perform academically. Realising, apparently, that straw did in fact help in the manufacture of bricks, he observed: "The majority of the classes inspected did very well and where the appearance made was less than satisfactory it was clear that no blame attached to the teacher. The (C) classes generally were weak and apparently unable to respond to instruction on the same level as other classes. It is therefore worthwhile considering whether in the intersts of the pupils themselves, a somewhat simpler syllabus would not be advantageous."

One indication of the predominance of the ability to pay to get the foot in the door, despite the abolition in 1918 of fees for the upper school, comes from the lists of admissions which include pupils' home addresses. Over a long period of time, and particularly in the fee paying years, these lists confirm that very many Academy pupils lived in the affluent Crown district.

Ability to pay, or lack of it, certainly influenced the attitudes of some staff to pupils in what was a fundamentally snobbish institution. Fee paying disappeared after World War 2 to be replaced by entry entirely on merit. So, during the 50s, did the primary department whose products also tended to be afforded elevated status by some teachers. But snobbery among a few older members of staff struggled on, arguably into the mid 60s, with the need to perpetuate a social elite temporarily invested in those from the Crown area or with influential parents.

One Royal Academy institution which has its origins in the early 1920s is the Howden Medals for Honour, awarded annually to the senior boy and girl deemed to have brought most credit to the School. These were first awarded in 1922 to William McKell and Agnes Smith.

Bill McKell, the son of the Drumnadrochit schoolmaster, spent much of his professional career in educational administration in Nigeria but returned to Inverness to retire and for many years thereafter fulfilled the function of the school's chief invigilator for external examinations.

However his own career as a Royal Academy pupil was not without incident. A log book entry dated June 21st 1921 records that: "A serious accident occurred in the playground today during the morning interval. Buxton Forsyth was struck by a heavy weight which was thrown by Wm. McKell in practising for the sports. All agree that the incident was entirely accidental. Buxton sustained a fractured skull and was successfully operated on this evening."

We can only speculate about the frame of mind in which the young McKell was left for the school sports the following afternoon, or for the Inter School Sports a week later at which those regular visitors to the Royal Academy, the La Scala and St. Abbans Trophies, were both won.

Magazines returned in the spring of 1925 after a lapse of more than a decade, broken only by the three war issues of "The Academical". This new generation of publications had a completely different slant to them. The "Academicals" of decades gone by had been creations of the Old Boys' Club, but now we have what can genuinely be called a School Magazine. The first School Magazine (known in brief as the I.R.A.M.) appeared in April 1925 with a cover price of one penny although this soon doubled. These early magazines give a valuable insight into school life at the time.

Royal Academy Guide Company - 1926 - 27

Athletic Notes

3rd INVERNESS (ACADEMY) GUIDES.

Guide parades have been held in the gymnasium regularly every week this session and have been well attended. We were all glad to welcome Miss Roy back again after her long illness, and also our new Lieutenant—Miss Horne. Early in January we held an enrolment when a number of recruits made their promises and were presented with their badges by Mrs Morrison. The ceremony, which was witnessed by several parents and visitors, was presided over by the Rector.

At the end of April we were inspected by Miss Maclean, Rossal, District Commissioner, who expressed great satisfaction at the smartness and, particularly, the jolliness of the company.

This term we have all been working feverishly for the Guide fete, which is to be held in the grounds of Muirtown House on June 15th. We are sure the "intervals" of many have been sweetened by partaking of home-made toffee manufactured by the Guides. It is to be hoped that pupils, parents, and staff will patronise the fete liberally, and succumb to the joys of hoop-la, fortune-tellers, etc., etc.

The Academy Guides have the honour of being chosen to perform the Camp-Fire ceremony at the fete, and they are also to sing and dance. We hope these performances, the product of much labour, will be witnessed by a large section of the school.

Great excitement was caused among the younger members of the company by the fact that we had our photograph taken for publication in the I.R.A.M. Perhaps their excitement will abate somewhat when they see the result on another page of this issue. We are afraid that the "3rd Inverness" is not a thing of beauty although it may be a joy for ever.

At present we are all looking forward with great eagerness to that mecca of all guides—camp. We are to spend ten days under canvas at Rosemarkie at the beginning of July, and already the mere thought of it has cheered many a weary Guide in the throes of a quarterly examination. Visitors will be welcome on Wednesday, July 6th. Please bring your own tea.

We believe that several members of the company are heroically practising eating porridge in preparation for that time, while others are living in hope that Miss Roy will forget to order the oatmeal.

The company would like to heartily thank Miss Roy and Miss Horne for the very hard work they have put in to ensure our meetings being the jolly times they are, and also for spending so much of their leisure time in rehearsing our performances for the bazaar.

Guide Report - 1927

From 1927 onwards they contain photographs in addition to text and adverts, and this photographic source has been drawn on extensively in this and later chapters. Photos of sports teams were taken at the old Playing Field at Ardross Street, with the hostel clearly visible in the background. Also of particular interest is the photo of the Royal Academy company of Girl Guides which existed for many years in the town.

The June 1926 Magazine contains a much more detailed list than usual of School Sports results, right down to individual times and distances. Of particular interest here is the comprehensive all round performance of the intermediate Champion Ian C. Young - arguably the greatest sportsman ever to have come

CHRISTMAS NUMBER.

The Inverness Royal Academy Magazine

Vol. IV. No. 1.   DECEMBER 1928.   Price 6d

MAGAZINE COMMITTEES.
EDITORIAL COMMITTEE.

EMILY SCOTT.	WILLIAM R. DARNLEY.
KATHERINE E. MACKENZIE.	Mr J. H. ANDERSON-ROBERTSON.
ARCHIBALD M. DOBBIE.	Mr A. J. HOUSTON.
WILLIAM MATHESON.	Mr A. A. WALKER.
CHARLES DOUGHERTY.	Mr D. J. MACDONALD.

COLLECTING COMMITTEE.

MARGARET JACK.	ERNEST M. DARNLEY.
KATIE M. MACQUEEN.	JAMES A. CHALMERS.
DONALD F. MELVEN.	Mr A. A. WALKER.

Mr A. J. HOUSTON.

BUSINESS COMMITTEE.

Art Editor—Mr J. S. D. JOHNSTON.
News Column—BESSIE M. MACKENZIE.
CECIL ROSS.
ALASTAIR ROSS.
Mr J. S. D. JOHNSTON.

Advertisements—DONALD R. BEATON.
CONSTANCE M. SIMMIE.
JOHN H. MACDONALD.
Publishing—GEORGE M. COONEY.
Distribution—BETTY M. MACDONALD.

Mr D. J. MACDONALD.

---

out of Inverness.

Ian Young was a member of the family which owned the local drapery firm of Young and Chapman which began life on Church Street but later moved to the Union Street site occupied at the time of writing by Arnotts. He was a phenomenal sprinter, and while the times indicated in the 1926 results are not perhaps outstanding for a boy in the middle years in school, we have no way of knowing what the weather and ground conditions were like on the day - nor whether he was even exerting himself.

By 1934 Ian Young was good enough to win Empire Games bronze medals for Scotland in the 100 yards and the 4 x 110 yards relay and the following year he claimed the Scottish Native record for the 100 yards. However it seems that technology had not yet caught up with him, as he recalled in a conversation with the author for a feature in the "Inverness Courier" in November 1990.

"In these days wind gauges were never heard of and it was a bit breezy

that day. In my heat of the 100 I recorded 9.9 seconds and won the final in 9.8 seconds, both performances being better than the old (Scottish Native) record. The only way officials could estimate the wind was by looking at the flags and guessing. In the end the SAAA decided to accept my 9.9 seconds as a record but not the 9.8. I still have mixed feelings about that because a gauge might have shown my faster time to be acceptable - but on the other hand it might have ruled out what I did get."

the 1920s

Because there was no athletic club in Inverness until 1947, Ian Young joined Edinburgh Harriers while doing his drapery apprenticeship in the city in 1929. But when he returned to Inverness to work in the family firm, it was at his old school's recently acquired playing fields at Millburn that he trained for his most important races of 1934 and 1935.

In 1936 he was selected for Great Britain at the Berlin Olympics where he might have come face to face with the great Jesse Owens, but it was not to be.

"That September (1935) my father took ill and I was called upon to take over the management of the business. Very soon afterwards a letter arrived, informing me that I had been selected for Britain at both the 100 and 220 yards

---

Inverness' Most Popular Shops.

The Mothers of the Academy Pupils, their Mothers and Grandmothers for the past thirty years, have been Customers of

YOUNG & CHAPMAN'S.

Nowhere else can they be so satisfactorily and cheaply suited with their Daughters' Academy Outfits, Gym Suits, Gym Tunics, Gym Hose, Party and Dance Frocks, Jumpers, Blazers, Hats, Tams, Waterproofs, Ties, &c. INSPECTION CORDIALLY INVITED.

Young & Chapman,
23 and 29 Church Street, ... Inverness.

the 1920s *for the 1936 Olympics in Berlin. But on the advice of the family doctor I decided I could not leave my father with the responsibility of the shop for the six weeks I would be away - so I had to turn the selection down and I never ran again after that."*

Ian Young continued to manage the business until 1952 when it was sold and he left Inverness to settle first in Suffolk and latterly in Devon where he became honorary president of Dartmouth AC.

It is very easy to take for granted the realities of the present or the manner in which history has occurred without considering how dependent such things sometimes are on single, extremely finely balanced events. Human experience is littered with instances where, but for a single, marginal outcome, matters might have turned out quite differently.

One such instance is the "damned close run thing" of the Battle of Waterloo and how European history might have unfolded had Napoleon won. On a more modest scale, the future of Inverness Royal Academy may well have been radically altered by the untimely death in 1929 at the age of just 45 of James H. Anderson Robertson, Principal Teacher of English. He simply went to Glasgow during the Christmas holidays to compete in the Scottish chess championships, contracted pleurisy and died in a nursing home there on January 19th.

Had he, as was being predicted with increasing confidence before an unexpected relapse, survived the attack, he might have gone on to occupy his post for another 20 years. The fact that he did not opened up an opportunity for promotion for one Donald John MacDonald who might otherwise have had to take his considerable talents elsewhere. The rest, as they say, is history.

The son of a Glasgow minister, Anderson Robertson studied his subject at Wadham College Oxford and joined the staff of the Royal Academy in 1908. A tribute from a former pupil recollects how he refused to accept the orthodoxy which restricted the study of poetry to Palgrave's Golden Treasury but extended the scope of his classes to cover contemporary poets as well. He also formed the Mermaid Club for pupils and this met weekly at his home on Victoria Terrace to read academic papers and hold scholarly debates.

Other interests included the production of plays and the revival of the school cricket club. Despite a susceptibility to attacks of asthma, which had caused him to be invalided out of the army during the war, he had a great interest in sport. He was also not averse to going ice skating at the popular venue of Loch na Sanais below Torvean Hill one day and deriving from that the inspiration for an English lesson the next. (Incidentally there is at least one reference in the log to the school being closed for a half day in winter simply to allow ice skating.)

Then there was the school magazine to which Anderson Robertson made such a leading contribution in the four years since its reappearance. The issue of April 1929 was fulsome in its praise of him, with no fewer than four separate articles, including the leader and tributes from both staff and pupils.

But although the school at the end of the 1920s lost one of its institutions among the staff, the next decade would provide ample evidence of its ability to create an abundance of new legends. Many of the recruits of the 30s would keep Midmills stocked with "characters" and "worthies" until the building ended its links with Inverness Royal Academy and indeed until the teaching profession seemed no longer to have a place for such personalities.

It therefore appears fitting that the magazine of July 1929 should have informed the school: "Many of our readers will be familiar with the university career of Miss Elizabeth Thomson. They will be pleased to learn that she has obtained an appointment in Manchester High School for Girls."

But not for long. There seems little doubt that the individual referred to here is the brilliant Dux of 1924 known to her friends as Betty Thomson and simply as "Jess" to pupils in the course of a career of over 40 years at Inverness Royal Academy which was to start early in 1931.

the 1930s

Education was certainly not exempted from the ravages of the global economic depression of the early 1930s and in September 1931 the log book records: "The Rector absent attending a conference with the Secretary for Scotland on the reduction in teachers' salaries to meet the present financial difficulties in the country."

Similar moves against the Navy sparked off a mutiny in the Fleet at Invergordon but life seems to have gone on as normal at the top of Stephen's Brae despite the economic decline. Indeed one former pupil seems to have had a clearer grasp of the situation than most. Buxton Forsyth must have made a full recovery from the fractured skull inflicted accidentally by Bill McKell's shot putting efforts in 1921. Eleven years later he won first prize in the Scottish bankers' essay competition on the subject "An account of the Economic Crisis of 1931." Buxton was the son of the former head of the school's Modern Languages department Mr. A.R. Forsyth.

But despite strains on the public purse, the previously high levels of educational scrutiny certainly seem to have been maintained in these difficult times. Although there may have been moves to reduce cash available to pay teachers, the Government still seems to have been able to fund very regular visits by H.M. Inspectors, and also by external examiners. No less than seven different HMIs are recorded as having visited the school to inspect or to examine during the second half of session 1930 - 31.

A battalion of other examiners included well known local minister the Rev. Ernest J. F. Elliott of St. Columba High Church who made a number of visits to appraise Scripture Knowledge. Local ministers appeared invariably satisfied with their regular examinations of Religious Instruction. In 1936 the Rev. Alexander Boyd headed a posse of three clergymen and observed that: "The children showed intimate knowledge of the portions of Scripture professed and the memory work was exceedingly well rendered." In an era when "R.I." and the rote learning of Scripture were still not beyond being taught with the Bible in one hand and the belt in the other, that might very well have been the case.

The log book gives the impression of a constant stream of Inspectors, Examiners and Managers making their way through the school to the extent that greeting and entertaining them must have taken up a great deal of the Rector's time.

Their reports are generally good, with Mr. Gilbert Watson's remarks on Latin, also referred to in the previous chapter, conspicuous among the few

LABORE ET VIRTUTE.

The steeple clock gives note of parting day,
The shopboy whistles gayly—he is free.
The schoolboy homeward drags his weary way,
And seeks some solace in a cup of tea.

Then rising from the table full of woe,
With sorrowful and sheer exhausted looks,
Into a quiet and dismal room he'll go,
And pore upon his wretched pile of books.

For four long hours he labours, lost in thought,
Nor looks at aught except his weary work;
This is the price of knowledge dearly bought,
By those who must not grumble, must not shirk.

Not until bedtime ends his working day,
Till morning, many hours do not remain;
Then, toiling hard, ascending "Stephen's Brae,"
His tedious tasks begin all o'er again.

ANON., V.b.

THE HAPPY LAND.

There is a happy land,
Down Stephen's Brae,
Where we get nice hot pies
Once every day.
Oh! how the scholars yell,
When they hear the "Inty" bell!
Oh! how they run "pell-mell"
Down Stephen's Brae.
You'll see them standing there
In a huge big queue;
To go into the shop
To get their "daily due."
Oh! how the scholars yell,
When they hear the "Inty" bell!
Oh! how they run "pell-mell,"
Down Stephen's Brae.

AMY GOLLAN, Class III.b.

Magazine poetry - early 30s

exceptions. However unlike modern reports they are overwhelmingly subject based and make scant reference to the school's management and overall strategies.

In August 1931, the following comments were made: "The younger secondary classes are all making favourable progress in the study of French...... Work of high merit has been accomplished in all the classes taking this subject (German)........ In mathematics the instruction is highly successful at every point...... The instruction in art is vigorous and progressive.... This year for the first time, presentations were made in commercial subjects. The general impression produced by inspection of the work was very favourable....... In cookery the pupils show facility in manipulation and the pracitcal work is good." In addition, Miss Kennedy's primary department continued to receive glowing reports and inspections of Inverness Royal Academy have continued in similar terms right up to the present day.

However on a more mixed note (and this is also quoted verbatim): "Although the results in English are not yet all that may be desired there is this year a quite definite improvement which is as gratifying as it is deserved. The English staff has worked faithfully and one feels certain that their work will

the 1930s

ultimately receive the measure of success at which they aim."

It is perhaps slightly ironic that in his comment on English of all subjects, the unnamed Inspector should commit an apparent grammatical faux pas. In the second sentence he uses the singular form of the verb i.e. "the staff has worked" in advance of the plural pronouns "their" and "they".

But the message which this comment seems to convey is that the English department was certainly on a steep improvement curve. That in turn seems perfectly in tune with the fact that D.J. MacDonald, of whom much more later, should have inherited the Principal Teachership just two years previously and was clearly making his presence felt.

AUSTIN TEN SALOON
£172 10/-

As DISTRIBUTORS of AUSTIN, MORRIS, M.G., WOLSELEY RILEY, DAIMLER, LANCHESTER, SUNBEAM, TALBOT and other Cars, and ALBION, AUSTIN and MORRIS Commercial Vehicles, we cordially invite you to inspect our stock of New 1934 Models at 36 ACADEMY STREET, INVERNESS, where Cars are available for Demonstration. Our Salesmen will inspect and make you an offer for your Present Car in Part Exchange for a New One.

You are bound to be interested in the NEW AUSTIN HAYES GEARLESS TRANSMISSION, which will here be Demonstrated FOR THE FIRST TIME IN SCOTLAND.

Let us arrange for YOUR TRIAL RUN ON THIS CAR or any other in which you are interested.

Macrae & Dick Ltd
MOTOR ENGINEERS,
INVERNESS
&
NAIRN.

PHONE:- INVERNESS 7 and 8.   PHONE:- NAIRN 4.

Mr. Watson's report on Latin, although once again critical, does give a hint of ongoing improvement. He begins: "The continued weakness of some of the Latin classes makes it necessary to report with some detail re this subject." After one and a half pages, which bring the junior classes out in a more favourable light than the senior, he concludes with the observation: "For this purpose, thorough and systematic revision of the school written work is essential."

Interestingly enough the 1932 report, apparently made by a different inspector, is rather less damning and reports on Latin from later in the 30s are very much more positive.

This was the departmental environment into which Miss Jessie E. Thomson, M.A. 1st class honours Classics, Edinburgh would have been introduced when she joined the staff on 9th January 1931. Jess, who was an outstanding dux in 1924, was just one of a number of Royal Academy legends who joined the staff in the early 30s.

Many of them gave the school long and devoted service, often in their own peculiar way, with the most flexible of interpretations of that last adjective perfectly permissible in some cases. Service lasting over 30 years was by no means uncommon and there were many new recruits during the 30s. This meant that for good or ill there was created here a considerable nucleus of staff who taught right through the 40s and 50s and well into the 60s.

Jess did not retire until 1972, by which time she had given Inverness Royal Academy over forty years of her life. She was part of a generation of characters and worthies who, over the last two or three decades, have more or less entirely disappeared from the teaching profession.

Possibly the last of that particular generation was Maude Yule (Maude Anderson after she got the husband in the wake of the fur coat and the car, her much publicised three fold aim in life) who was my own first Physics teacher in the 60s. She took up her post on August 29th 1939 - three days later Hitler invaded Poland. Her departure in 1979 marked the end of an era in more respects than the end of Midmills as a home for the School.

Others who arrived in the early 30s include Tom Fraser, initially as assistant to Mr. Pealling in the Science Department and latterly succeeding him at its helm. "Tomuck's" departure came in 1966 after 36 years. Janet K. (Duggie) Douglas did considerable supply teaching in the late 20s and well into the 30s before formally joining the Modern Languages department. She did not depart until 1965, only to return the following session, once again in a supply capacity. Then there was Buckie whose 36 year love affair with Inverness Royal Academy began in 1934.

The Maths department was strengthened during the decade by two new faces. Ethel C. Forbes, who ended her career as a much respected Lady Superintendent, joined as an assistant teacher in August 1932. Then Leslie "Pop" Frewin became Principal Teacher in succession to Charles Mitchell in April 1934 before eventual promotion to Second Master. He also ran the hostel at Drummond Park, retired in the early 60s and died in 1999, aged 96. Later in the 30s there would be the arrival of Ellis Stewart (Curly, but apparently known earlier as "Ginger") whose career in Modern Languages would, like those of many others, be interrupted by distinguished war service. Many of these teachers have already been referred to in this book's predecessor "Up Stephen's Brae" and many will appear once again later in this text.

There were departures too, including Miss Rhoda MacLeod the infant

CLASS VIa., 1933-34.

Whyte] [Inverness

Back row (l. to r.)—J. A. Duthie, A. M. Macdonald, Ina Ross, D. Macaulay.
Standing (l. to r.)—J. R. Cowieson, R. I. Morrison, M. Macdonald, C. Woodward, E. W. King, M. O. Fisher, D. Matheson, D. K. A. Mackenzie.
Sitting (l. to r.)—A. J. Munro, S. M. Wilson, M. R. Kerr, E. Morrison, E. B. S. Duguid, L. McIntosh, F. Jefferies, B. Tolmie, H. Murphy, I. Campbell, G. Campbell.

mistress who had joined the staff in 1895 and stayed for 39 years.

On the subject of longserving members of staff, the retirals of Principal Teachers of English and Music in the 1990s meant that in almost concurrent 84 year periods, both these departments had just four heads. In the first case, James Anderson Robertson (1908-29), D.J. MacDonald (1929-1944) and Jacob Mowat (Fritz) (1944-68) preceded Eddie Hutcheon (1968-92). In Music, Lewis Owen ran the department from 1912-40 and Lawrence Rodgers until 1963. Ian Bowman, the shortest serving of all eight staff, was in charge for a mere decade after that and Anne MacIntyre was Principal Teacher from 1973 until 1996.

Returning to matters concerning pupils, this was a time when alcohol abuse (or even use) was clearly of considerable concern and in the early 1930s there are references to "Temperance Lectures" to various classes. "Temperance" - which means moderation - has tended to be interpreted by those promoting it as "total abstinence". At a time when prohibition and veto polls leading to "dry" areas were high on the public agenda, it is certainly interesting to speculate what the tone of these lectures may have been.

There are also stark reminders that medical science was still in a rudimentary form in the 1930s. In one dreadful, albeit not very typical, 17 month period between March 1932 and August 1933, no fewer than eight pupils died, at least two of them as a result of appendicitis and one from the complications of rheumatic fever. Particularly distressing was the passing of one third year pupil on 23rd March 1932 following an accident playing football in the playground.

In March 1931 a flu epidemic swept through the school. It appears to have begun early in the month and absences peaked at 29% on the 11th. Eight days later there was still a 19% absence rate although the epidemic seems to have petered out after that. Outbreaks of various diseases were still not uncommon in the 30s, although it is the flu epidemic which followed World War 1 which has probably achieved the greatest notoriety

In 1936 and 1937 there are regular references to pupils and staff having to be quarantined due to scarlet fever and chicken pox. Scarlet fever reared its head at Drummond Park boys' hostel where a case was found in March 1937, leading to a number of pupils being excluded from school for ten days. These included Alistair Cameron, James Muir, Ronald Macdonald, Ronald J. Macdonald, Donald J. MacLean and Iain Macdonald whose sitting of Leaving Certificates was affected. The other examinations, to which there is abundant reference at the time but which have now long gone, are the Third Year Control and the Promotion Control.

the 1930s

By this time two hostels were in operation - Drummond Park for the boys and Hedgefield for the girls - with the Ardross Street premises vacated for use as the County Buildings. This made a lot of sense because these new premises, Hedgefield in particular, were much handier for access to the school. And that was how things remained for pupils from outlying areas and the islands until Inverness Royal Academy stopped taking them in the late 70s.

Drummond Park already had a place in local folklore from the days around the turn of the century when it had belonged to a Mrs. Playne Smith. This particular lady created an annual Inverness institution by dispensing a Christmas dram to local cabbies who would queue up her drive in their horsedrawn conveyances to receive their tipple before trotting away in search of more fares. Public spirited it may have seemed at the time, but nowadays it is all a million miles away from Northern Constabulary's festive drink-drive purges. Now they would be giving Mrs. Playne Smith's premises a great deal of attention indeed, to the probable extent of mounting a standing breathalyser patrol on Drummond Road.

During the Easter holidays of 1935, Andrew Harrow Watson, the school's janitor for 41 years, died after a period of ill health. It must have been Mr. Watson whom Robin Denoon took to be the Rector when she first arrived at the school in the early 1920s. Andrew Watson was another Royal Academy legend who apparently had an incredible facility with the school's idiosyncratic coal fired heating system. Although chanelling hot water to radiators in some rooms still defeated Watson, he seems to have been much more successful in this respect than his successor. On

Andrew Harrow Watson

December 13th 1937, Mr. Crampton Smith recorded: "A very cold day *and the temperature of many of the rooms was below 40F*. Closed 1pm." (Author's italics!) There are also memories of Mrs. Watson looking after the little girls in the Junior School, helping them on and off with their shoes on cold winter days.

On 22nd January 1936 "The school assembled in the hall at 9:55 to hear a broadcast of the Proclamation of King Edward VIII at St. James's Palace." Two days later the building was closed for three hours for the Proclamation by the Sheriff to be heard in the town and it was closed all day on the 28th for the funeral of King George V. At the other end of that year, there is no reference at all in the log book to the abdication of the same Edward VIII.

On 12th May 1937 there was a further holiday for the coronation of George VI. The previous day, three town councillors visited the school to present each pupil with a bronze medal and a box of chocolate. And, possibly as compensation for not having been able to demonstrate his patriotism on the track in the 1936 Olympics, Ian Young presented each child in the Primary Department with "a flag" - there is little doubt as to which kind!

The generation who were pupils in the 1930s were also the generation on which the brunt of the fighting of the Second World War would fall. As teenagers they would have watched unfold before their eyes the catalogue of errors, unsound judgements and unfulfilled hopes on the part of politicians which ultimately led to the catastrophe which engulfed civilisation at the end of the decade.

However it is all very well, with the benefit of hindsight, to analyse the follies of the 1930s in the manner in which we do nowadays. From the perspective of those living at the time, it must have been a lot more difficult to believe that, with the "war to end all wars" still a relatively recent and terrible memory, the scene was being set for another altogether more dreadful whirlwind.

So as Germany elected its Nazi government and callously broke its post war treaty commitments, they watched from a distance and still studied Horace, Virgil and Chaucer at the top of Stephen's Brae. And as Fascist forces inexorably established themselves in various locations in Europe and Africa, the games of rugby, football, shinty and hockey went on apace at the new War Memorial playing field which opened in 1933 at Millburn.

That particular facility was soon to be graced by a superb new pavilion which for over 40 years would accommodate Royal Academy "field" classes and extra curricular activities. After the final departure from Midmills in 1979, Millburn Academy, which opened in the early 1960s and had since shared the field, took it over completely along with the pavilion.

The New Pavilion

At this point the traditional access from Victoria Drive was closed and the short, stony brae down to the field itself, where bicycles were parked for so many years, quickly became overgrown. In the mid 1990s severe doubts were expressed about the future serviceability of the rapidly decaying pavilion. However it was still in use (to accommodate visiting Royal Academy football teams as it happens) at least as late as the end of 1998.

the 1930s

School Sports - 1935

The 1930s appears to have been a particularly active decade on the sports field, if coverage in school magazines is anything to go by. And there was no hiding place for team members, whose performances were thoroughly scrutinised and reviewed publicly and sometimes mercilessly in magazines.

One other remarkable feature of the 30s, and the latter years of the decade in particular, is the manner in which fashions and hairstyles seem to put 20 years on teenagers. In so many of the photos from magazines of the period, 18 year old boys in particular look uncannily close to 40!

It is perhaps time that the Primary Department, or Junior School received a little prominence. Although part of Inverness Royal Academy and a major

the 1930s

source of pupils for the Secondary school, it was very separate in many respects. It had its own dedicated wing and its own Principal Teacher who was responsible to the Rector and a staff who were very much kept at arm's length by many of their secondary colleagues.

Elizabeth Chalmers taught an infant class there between 1937 and 1939 and has a crystal clear recollection of what the place was like. The following is a condensed version of a lengthy conversation I had with her about life in the Junior school in the 1930s.

"I had previously taught for four years in the Dem. School attached to Moray House in Edinburgh but I saw this advert for a Froebel trained teacher of infants, which I was, and I also had an Infant Mistress endorsement. It was a considerable culture shock to come up here because there were many differences. For a start in Edinburgh, classes had been right up at the maximum size of 45 whereas at the Academy each had just over 20 children. On the other hand in Edinburgh I just had to ask for materials and I got them whereas here I remember going to "Jake" Johnson to request material for art and all I got for my entire class was a roll of sticky paper.

We had very little to do with the senior school - we were quite separate and they looked down on us. The two staffs did not mingle too much and we were beneath the notice of the senior school. When I came up here I had to find digs and got a room in Lovat Road. Mr. Graham the Gaelic master also stayed there and you might have thought he would have taken me in tow on the first day. But he actually ate in the dining room while I ate in the kitchen so I didn't stay too long there. It was Nivvie, whose sister had ben on the leet for my job and was in the upper school herself, who actually greeted me and made me feel at home.

There were seven Junior staff and of course Miss Kennedy took what we would now call Primary 7 while her number two Alice Grant took the next class down. Along with Miss MacRae and Miss MacLean who took the next oldest classes, they all had rooms on the left hand side of the long corridor which ran from the entrance at the front to the Junior assembly hall at the back, looking out on the playground. Miss Kennedy, who was a very powerful lady, had the last before the hall. On the other side, looking inwards, were the rooms where Florence Hoare who was very clever indeed and Carol Barratt the infant mistress and I had our rooms and there was also a cloakroom. I had the very youngest class and when they only came in for the morning I would take Miss Barratt's older class for handwork in the afternoon.

We also had our separate staff room at the front end of the corridor. The women's staffroom for the senior school was on the first floor of the main

Mary Wilson
Hockey Captain, 1930 -31

D C R Wilson
Cricket Captain 1936

D McGillivray
Rugby Captain , 1935 -36

Joyce Ross
Hockey Captain, 1936 - 37

the 1930s

building above Miss McGill the Secretary's office at the front. We did not go there but I believe there used to be a battle royal to see who got the basket chair. In these days it was very formal and we were not on first name terms - it was always 'Miss Kennedy, Miss MacRae or Miss Grant' or whatever.

It was a happy school because they were all the same kind of children who were very well behaved and were used to going to each other's homes. If you said 'sit down and fold your arms' they sat down and folded their arms. The school was still fee paying and they were predominatly from professional families and many lived close to the school in the Crown. It was all fairly formal. You stood in front teaching and at the end of the week you wrote up your log.

The only problem I remember was when there were two brothers and one was brighter than the other but there was a bit of a fuss that one was not doing so well. I had an awful job persuading 'Crampie' that this simply happened in families and you couldn't just expect the two to be the same.

Mr. Crampton Smith, or 'Crampie' as he was called, wore rubber soled boots and he would creep along the corridor and peek through your window to see what you were doing. In complete contrast with D.J. Crampie had no presence at all and you did not really feel you got very much support from him.

I married in the spring of 1939 and in these days that meant you were out. Married women just could not stay on in teaching but the war changed all that because they were very glad to get anybody they could."

However Mrs. Chalmers' association with Inverness Royal Academy was by no means finished at that point because her two children Murray and Charlotte both became pupils there, Murray becoming Dux in 1957, and Charlotte Girl Captain in 1961.

There is little evidence of much awareness of the darkening European political situation in any account of school life. The subject of the Ettles Lecture of 1932 by Randolph Churchill, son of that arch opponent of appeasement Winston Churchill, is not recorded, although at that point there still must have seemed little to fear.

The 1935 lecture on "Germany" was given by Lt. Col Stewart Roddie, an FP and son of the music master whose compositions had been such a prominent part of school concerts of the 1890s. Lt. Col. Roddie had been with the Allied Control Commission in Germany, set up as a result of the Treaty of Versailles of 1919, and recalled his experiences in the book "Peace Patrol". What he had to say in his lecture about the vast changes of the previous two or three years within Germany is again not noted. However his personal entry in the log book reads: "I visited this my old school today and shall carry away the memory of a development that I could scarcely have believed had I not seen it."

The rifle club seems to have enjoyed something of a revival as another conflict with Germany loomed. During the years of appeasement, interest seems to have waned but a report in the school magazine of April 1938 records a dramatic upturn. Within two or three years, many of these aspiring shots would be performing their craft for real on active service. And those who, for whatever reason, remained at home would soon be in a rather better position than most to contemplate Churchill's advice that "you can always take one with you!"

On September 27th 1938, Prime Minister Neville Chamberlain broadcast to the nation during his spell of what we now call "shuttle diplomacy" which led to the Munich agreement which in turn allowed Germany to annexe the Sudetenland from Czechoslovakia. He said: "How horrible, fantastic, incredible it is that we should be digging trenches and trying on gas masks because of a quarrel in a far away country between people of whom we know nothing!" Ironically on that very same day, Mr. Owen, the Principal Teacher of Music, is recorded as being absent on ARP duties.

The editorial of the December 1938 School Magazine (overleaf) gives a chillingly vivid insight into the naive hopes of continuing peace to which many still clung, despite belated preparations for war. The complete disregard for the fate of the Czechoslovaks is more or less identical to Mr. Chamberlain's.

However the hope was a vain one. The new session opened on August 29th 1939 with Messrs. Black and MacLeay already absent on military duty and on September 1st 1939, with Hitler's Panzers already violating Poland and war inevitable, the school was closed for ten days for the reception of 900 evacuees from Edinburgh. Their distribution to homes in the Culduthel and Culcabock districts, which followed a meal at the school, was supervised by Royal Academy staff.

War broke out on Sunday, September 3rd 1939 as Elizabeth Chalmers was attending St. Columba High Church. It was the first day of of what would turn out to be a 50 year spell as a Sunday School teacher there. She has a clear recollection of John Edgar (of Edgar the Baker's who married the first ever girl Howden Medallist Ruth Smith) having the then unusual asset of a radio in his car. He left the congregation to listen to Mr. Chamberlain announce at 11.15 am that "this country IS at war with Germany", and conveyed the distressing news to the Rev. Elliott who duly informed the congregation.

The brief prelude of the Phoney War was at hand, but the next decade would not be very old before the fighting began in earnest and those who were pupils and teachers by day would become firewatchers on the school roof by night.

THE INVERNESS ROYAL ACADEMY MAGAZINE

DECEMBER 1938   VOL. XIV.   NO. 1

THE EDITOR'S CHAIR

It is the custom for the Editorial of a new session to concern itself mainly with hopes and petitions for the well-being of its forthcoming issues. We respect tradition; the policy of past editors is above our reproach; but a greater matter lies still freshly in our minds, and demands priority.

We have all been relieved by the signing of the Munich Agreement. The years 1914-18 abundantly proved to us the futility of conflict, the barbarity of war, and yet, within a short time of the Peace Treaties a similar devastation was threatening us. All we had fought for in the last war, all we had learned, seemed about to be overthrown.

But now the storm has passed over our heads. We have gone back to our textbooks and examination papers with the knowledge that a difficult problem has been solved, not by wholesale slaughter, but by conference and discussion. We have paid a high price for peace in the sacrifice of Czechoslovakia, but surely this loss of territory is far, far better than a savage destruction of countless thousands of human lives.

To the untiring work of British and French politicians we owe much. To Czechoslovakia, for the noble sacrifice her people have made in the interests of European peace, we owe more. Born several years after the war, we know little of its actual horrors, but we have felt its influence, and, as we take up our books, we grow increasingly grateful to the men who have saved us from another conflict from which some of us might never have returned.

the 1940s

When school reopened for the Easter term on 8th January 1940, the most immediate concern was completely unrelated to the war which by now was four months old. Eighteen radiators had burst throughout the building, causing considerable flooding. It was a lot better than bombs bursting, although there had been precious little of that anywhere during this exceptionally cold winter of the Phoney War. Neither side had gone to that extent yet, the RAF preferring to drop propaganda leaflets over Germany instead while rival armies glowered at each other across the Siegfried and Maginot Lines.

However with the general fear that "the bomber will always get through", the Home Front was much more evidently at war now than between 1914 and 1918 and at an early stage Inverness Royal Academy was identified as a rest centre in the event of aerial bombardment. War charities had been quickly organised too and on 18th January 1940 the school held a concert in their aid in the huge Empire Theatre. It was a sell out and would be followed by many other, similar activities.

It was not until 4th March 1941, well into the period of the London blitz, that firewatching arrangements were put into operation. Mr. Crampton Smith instructed that: "There will be on duty every night from 6pm until 7:30 am, from Saturday at 12 noon and all day on Sunday either the janitor (or groundsman), a male member of staff and two girls over 16 years of age, or, the Janitor, two female members of staff and three boys over 16 years of age. Light refreshments to be supplied."

A number of members of staff had already left for war service. Apart from Messrs. Black and MacLeay, referred to in the previous chapter, there was also Ellis Stuart, destined to work under cover behind enemy lines for MI5, Charles Dougherty and Douglas Martin although Mr. Martin was to return to the school, having been invalided out of the army.

Along with many, many former pupils, they served with distinction. Inevitably news of casualties close to the school caused a great deal of distress, but few more than 2nd Lieut. J. Alastair Duthie of the Camerons who was killed in action against Rommel's forces in Libya in December 1941.

Alastair Duthie, second son of Second Master Alex. Duthie, had been a brilliant dux in 1934. He first became a pupil in the Primary Department at the age of five and continued his association with the school while a student at St. Andrews University by covering his father's classes during the latter's quite frequent absences.

It was said that his father, whose health seems to have been particularly

the 1940s

bad during the early 1940s in any case, was extremely hard hit by his loss. However despite ongoing absences, he carried on until he reached the age limit for retiral of 65 in June 1942 when he departed along with Miss Kennedy who had ruled the Primary Department for almost 30 years.

Mr. Duthie, whose other son Ian became Regius Professor of English Literature at Aberdeen University in 1954, died at the beginning of 1946. Also departing in the summer of 1942 was Miss Paterson who for 20 years had been matron in charge of the girls' hostel.

Alexander Duthie was succeeded as Second Master by Principal Teacher of English D.J. MacDonald while Miss Alice Grant took over as what would be the last head of the Primary Department.

One grievous loss within the staff resulted from the death in October 1940 of Lewis Owen, Principal Teacher of Music since 1912. He appears to have taken ill during the October long weekend and underwent surgery on Tuesday 8th but died on the Saturday.

It was two months before Lawrence Rogers was appointed as his successor. "Boosey" (a reference to the music publishers rather than to any inclination to drink) eventually took up his post on 3rd February 1941 and held it for almost quarter of a century. In his latter days in harness, a quiz in a school magazine would say of this bespectacled musician: "Mr. _____ rides a rickety, racketty bike and smokes a pipe." That indeed is how many will remember Boosey, riding along with his briefcase slung around the bar of the bicycle.

Later that year Maude's sister Gladys Yule, who became Mrs. Fairie, also joined the staff in the Art Department . She will be particularly remembered for her work in embroidering a fine lectern cloth with the school's coat of arms which is still in use.

But despite firewatching, the threat of bombing (which never became reality in Inverness), rationing, staffing disruptions and strain on accommodation due to the addition of evacuees to the roll, education marched on. On 13th October 1941, the Primary roll is recorded as 228 (including 16 evacuees) and the Secondary as 599 (including 34 evacuees) - a grand and still rapidly increasing total of 827 crammed into the first three phases of the building.

Following the abundance of photographic material from the 1930s there is very little from the 40s. When magazines reappeared in 1947 they were still, possibly due to post war shortages, photo free and those few photos which can be found in the archive are almost entirely prefects and sports teams. The only exception is this unnamed group of senior pupils,(opposite) perhaps one of the Sixth Year classes, and the sandbags betray it as a wartime snap.

An HMI report in October 1942 praised Inverness Royal Academy for its continuing effectiveness in these difficult times. It observed: "This large secondary school has naturally had its share of the strains inseparable from the conditions prevailing during a trying period of war activities, but in the capable hands of its devoted rector and his able staff, the school has been fortunate and the results of instruction continue, at all points, at the high level of former years. This is a notable achievement in the circumstances of the times. It is particularly gratifying that the Authority were able to secure the services of competent teachers whenever vacancies occurred, so enabling the corporate life of the school to be carried on with normal teaching power."

As an example of the disruption, the report later remarks that in the English Department "of the pre war permanent staff, only the Principal Teacher remains", although it fails to note that D.J. MacDonald now had the additional burden of Second Master's duties.

The school reopened in January 1943 with one absentee on the staff. "Nivvie" (Miss MacNiven) had become Mrs. MacDonald during the Christmas holidays and, far from being obliged to resign in these changed times, had been allowed three extra days off for a honeymoon.

That year there was a shortened summer break from 1st July to 3rd August,

the 1940s to accommodate an extra long "tattie holiday" when school was closed for the entire month of October to allow pupils to assist in taking in the crop. This arrangement continued in 1944 and 1945 when the high flying intellectual D. J., now the Rector, turned farm manager. His promotion appears to have included charge of the Royal Academy and High School "tattie howkers" which allowed him to be present only part time in the school.

Donald John MacDonald, almost inevitably in the view of many, succeeded William Crampton Smith when the latter retired at the beginning of 1944. Born in Lochcarron in 1900 and educated at the local school there, Dingwall Academy and Aberdeen University, "D.J." had joined the Royal Academy staff as an assistant teacher of English in 1924. Over the next 20 years he moved right through the ranks in the only school in which he ever taught, becoming Principal Teacher in 1929 and then second master, before rapidly aspiring to the top job.

He must have had a very busy life, holding very many offices outwith the school, including chieftain of the Gaelic Society of Inverness, chairman of the Northern Hospital Board of Management, president of the Inverness Battalion of the Boys' Brigade and elder of the West Church. He was also a member of the Rotary Club and on his election to that body, he recorded in the Log, with the greatest of propriety, that he would from then on, one afternoon a month, be late back to school after the customary Rotary lunch.

He was also very much the old style intellectual and frequently during public talks would preface literary references with statements like "you will remember what Gibbon said in 'The Decline and Fall of the Roman Empire'..... " when in practice most of his audience had never even heard either of the work or the author.

Even in his later years, by which time he had moved from his home in Green Drive to the Abbeyfield Residential Home in Crown Drive, he was sharp as a needle with total recall. I have an amazing memory of an interview I did for the BBC with an 85 year old D.J. at Abbeyfield when his recollections of New Year on the West Coast in the early years of the century were as stunningly vivid as they were brilliantly articulated. With the benefit of hindsight, the follow up should have been a 30 minute programme on his time at Inverness Royal Academy in which he would easily have held an audience singlehandedly for its entire duration.

For many years, almost up until his death in 1993, he kept very much in touch with the school, attending many functions and he also officially opened the school's Culduthel building in 1978. At Buckie's retiral presentation from the FPs' Association in 1970, the President David Wilson, in a reference to the presence of the previous rector, spoke of the Bible, Shakespeare and D.J., adding that one could be excused for thinking that the former were written by the latter.

His smallness of stature in no way detracted from the regard in which he was held and many of his former pupils speak of the "presence" he could command and a memory of that is included in the next chapter. D.J.'s promotion also created the need for a new Principal Teacher of English. Until the early 1970s it was perfectly permissible for individuals to hold two promoted posts at once and as a result, D.J. continued to run a department while he was second master, as did five of his successors. But his further elevation opened up a vacancy which was filled by the highly eccentric but at the same time extremely scholarly "Fritz".

Unfortunately the national paranoia about Fifth Columnists was still alive and well in 1944. So when Jacob Mowat arrived with the most guttural of Orcadian accents, which he never lost, the rumour machine jumped quickly to the idea that he was a German agent - hence the instant nickname. Fritz's eccentricities are already covered in "Up Stephen's Brae", but one of the letters I received after its publication did recollect the following, rather confusing method of getting a pupil to change seats: "You boy, in the back seat, in the front behind. Come up to the seat on the left behind the one to the right."

Names also rather confused Fritz to the extent that any girl from the Islands was inevitably referred to simply as "Morag".

Although the war had begun during the rectorship of Mr. Crampton Smith, it ended early in the 18 year tenure of D.J. MacDonald. The school duly gave thanks for deliverance from almost six years of strife when fighting concluded in Europe in May 1945 and with Japan in August.

As in 1914-18, the human cost was high. In World War 2,

W Crampton Smith

the 1940s

64 former pupils gave their lives which seems a lot compared with the 83 in the face of much higher overall casualty rates during the previous conflict. On the other hand the pre war school roll was much larger this time.

Of particular interest is the fact that a disproportionately large 28 of that 64 served with the RAF. One possible explanation may be that Inverness Royal Academy FPs would have been particularly well suited as Bomber Command aircrew among whom casualty rates were very high indeed. Extensive and sustained air attacks, mainly on Germany by night, made it statistically likely that aircrew would die before even completing a first standard tour of 30 operations.

Bomber Command was sending on these operations highly skilled, technically competent and educated young wireless operators, pilots, flight engineers and navigators. Many of those 28 FPs would have fitted that bill very well indeed among the 55,000 who made a disproportionate sacrifice on the part of the educated middle class as Bomber Harris vainly strove to bring Germany to its knees by air power alone.

Among the RAF casualties were Warrant Officer Alexander Fletcher and Sergeant Ian P. McHaffie Gordon, both pilots, and Air Gunner Alexander Murcar. Then there was Captain Harold Butterworth who was listed under the Royal Artillery but who was apparently lost on operations when serving with Bomber Command.

At least one F.P. appears to have survived the horrors of the trenches in the First War but succumbed in the Second. Hugh W. Corner M.D. M.R.C.P., one of the bank actuary's and his German wife's seven sons who served their country between 1899 and 1918, lost two brothers in 1915 while himself a lieutenant in the Camerons. He later qualified as a doctor and joined the RAF medical service in 1924, winning the Air Force Cross in 1941 and rising to the rank of Group Captain. He is described in the roll of honour as having met his death with Fighter Command the following year. This is tantalizingly enigmatic because while it was not unknown for senior officers to be lost on occasional flights as observers of bomber operations, another explanation apparently has to be sought in Group Captain Corner's case.

Men with a high degree of technical competence would also have been present among another large group of casualties, the nine Royal Artillerymen. These include Lieutenant Gordon Todd who was killed at the Anzio beachhead in 1944 and Major Hamish R. Wilson, drowned off Taranto in 1942.

Only twelve of the dead appear to have been footsoldiers. Apart from Alastair Duthie, they include Captain Roderick C. Matheson of the Indian Army, killed in the Far East, and Lieutenant Geoffrey Roberts of the Royal

Welch Fusiliers on the Normandy beach-head. This relative sparsity of infantrymen reflects the essential difference between the two world wars, and also the new demand outwith the infantry for the specific skills of educated young men - and women.

One of the many decorations awarded to FPs was the Vellum of the Royal Humane Society to Sub Lieutenant Allan Grant R.N. who drowned attempting to save a life in the River Tees in 1943.

Major General Denys Reid won the D.S.O., M.C. and Bar as a Captain in World War 1 and a Bar to his D.S.O. in Eritrea in 1940. He was later captured in the Western Desert but escaped and went on to command the 10th Indian Division in Italy, winning the C.B.E. in 1942.

The Rector's son, Surgeon Lieutenant Commander Alexander Crampton Smith was awarded the Croix de Guerre by the French for services during the capture of Elba and was also mentioned in Dispatches.

M.B.Es included Lieutenant Colonel Peter Donald, Rev. Gordon Fraser who was captured with so many other Highlanders at St. Valery in June 1940 and Captain Douglas Peterkin R.A.M.C. who helped evacuate 700 prisoners from Belsen in 1945.

The publication of school magazines was suspended in 1940 and it was 1947 before a Memorial issue appeared. This includes graphic articles from FPs who served in the Army, the Navy and the RAF. The contribution overleaf of an unnamed but typically highly educated airman is probably the best piece of writing I have seen during what has been lengthy scrutiny of a century of school magazines.

Apart from fulfilling a ceremonial function, this War Memorial issue publication also gives an admirable summary of what school life was really like during the seven years when there had been no regular magazines.

Some of the landmark occurrences such as appointments and retirals have been dealt with earlier in this chapter, but there is a lot of additional anecdotal wartime colour to be gleaned.

With "summer time" applying in winter, school did not open until 9:30 on the darkest days and there was also no bell to summon pupils in an era when bells were only to be used to warn of invasion. The building itself had become festooned with anti splinter netting, there were sandbags in the hall and Jake Johnston administered a rest centre in the building outside school hours. "Night life in the academic precincts became astonishing and various," the magazine records. The school gates went the way of all metal to produce tanks and battleships and there was a rapid contraction of the VIth form as they reached the age of conscription.

One pupil who remembers her seniors taking part in these firewatching

THE R.A.F.

We were coming up to the Dutch coast; a hundred and thirty miles to go to Bremen; I could see the light flak, winking, many coloured, organised for the benefit of a Hampden going in below us; lit threads of tracer were scoring the darkness out to starboard. A hundred and thirty to go, and all along there would be usual assortment — searchlights, night fighters, flak, variations on a disagreeable theme. I actually sat mathematics examinations to do this — for the privilege of wrestling with wind vectors, adjusting speeds, calculating heights and juggling with bomb sight settings, of being very frightened and uncomfortable.

It seemed a moot point whether I should be grateful to Room 7 and 13 and to Tommy Fraser's lab. Perhaps because I was going on leave, all being well, tomorrow, these thoughts, not usual in such circumstances, kept chewing round in my mind. Oh, well, 7 and 13 and the Labs had got me into this, maybe they would do the square thing and get me out: I should be needing some mathematical skill and precision in a minute or two if we were going to find the healthy road between Cuxhaven and Bremerhaven.

The slip stream of another bomber caught us and shook thoughts of other places out of me. We were coming up to Bremen; time to get the final settings on the bomb-sight, make the last check on wind velocity.

In minutes Bremen came up, just on the starboard bow; we were all right. It would be better to alter a few degrees south so that we could track down river to the target. It was plain that others had had the same idea, for the defences were, in the most literal sense, up and doing; a heavy barrage was concentrating along the bombing run of the first aircraft in.

Now it was our turn. I could feel the tension that seemed to hold the aircraft as well as its crew, as I passed the target course to the Captain. Right ahead now, as we turned on, the streets of Bremen were outlined and twinkling like children's sparklers as the first incendiaries took hold. Then, as the main weight of the attack came in, the whole place seemed to erupt in light, below. Above, in red, blue, green, yellow, the light flak and tracer crossed and wove in a web of fire.

The Oil Refinery on the left bank of the Weser was moving in the drift wires of my bomb sight. It was cold at 13,000 feet, but I could feel the itch of sweat running in my helmet, and my hands were sticky and "thumby" as I touched the bomb firing button. A searchlight exposed on us and held us, and as I lay on the perspex bombing panel I felt that to every battery below we must be the answer to the gunner's prayer; a fly stuck to the ceiling. The aircraft rocked and shivered as the shells found our height, but we lost the searchlight and steadied on our run, and I began to say my piece over the intercom., the part that the B.B.C. and the films made so familiar — "Bomb doors open; steady, steady; left, left; steady; bombs gone"—and the sudden lift that proved it, and the answering lift of the heart.

We came out across the enemy coast to the weary North Sea crossing, enlivened only by the early light; then the blessed sight of the Norfolk sands, and, behind, the dim patchwork of English fields.

The journey from East Anglia to London, the first step, was to be endured with impatience and sleep; what I wanted to hear was—"The train standing in Platform 13 is the 7.20 for Inverness, calling at Crewe and Perth." It was good to waken on the right side of the Border, to feel the wheels catch the points at Stanley and beat on Highland track. The hills at the head of the long Drumochter grades stood in grave welcome, as old friends — the county march, Glen Truim, Badenoch and Slochd, the last gateway of Home. Best of all, the Firth opening out from Culloden cutting, the first glimpse of the town, and, over the Black Isle, the long couchant bulk of Wyvis, viewed so many times on remembered afternoons of beatitude, whilst "unbending quietly" in Room 17.

On the morning before going back I went up to the School. It was a visit that, combined with seven days of Inverness and home, had always the most stabilising and reassuring effect on me. Rooms 9 and 7 were as industrious as ever, the Art Department was still keeping the blob running, and still apostrophising the H2S that whiffed up in volumes of offence from the labs. There was still the wide, peaceful grass, and the smell of turf and leaves at the playing fields. Here was something to hold by, that stayed put, and stayed sane.

On the afternoon train to London, going back, I had my affairs in perspective again.

duties is Nancy Scott, or Nancy Sutherland as she was known during her six years at the school from 1943-49. The daughter of a railway clerk, her only way to gain access to an academic education was by winning a bursary, fees being beyond the family means. However uniforms still had to be paid for by parents. She remembers a tremendous year for the Merkinch School where she was one of no fewer than 20 Academy bursars, fourteen of these being placed in Class 1A. This slightly upset the established preconception of social stratification which was alive and well at this time.

Unfortunately, as she revealed in an interview which is transcribed here, a bursary for the Academy was still not a guarantee of a long and thorough education.

"It was one thing to get the bursary, but a number of these pupils from the Merkinch area were very poor and their family circumstances forced them to leave school early to seek work so they didn't get the full benefit of such an education. Nevertheless they still did well and most climbed the ladders of promotion in later years.

Mr. Crampton Smith left shortly after I started at the Academy and therefore made little impact. D.J. certainly changed and revitalised the school. Younger and more dynamic, he quickly stamped his leadership on the establishment, but did he really need to appear dramatically from behind these curtains at assembly?

I also have fond memories of Tommy Fraser's science classes. It was a tradition that each year the Sixth Year boys would "dispose" of the tadpoles. Our boys chose to electrocute them during Tommy's absence - he never did determine the cause of their demise. There was also Charles Dougherty, Alan's father, who really made his pupils enjoy English while Frank Cunningham's geography classes were magic. He was one of the finest teachers I encountered and his later professorship was well deserved. Frank also ran outdoor club expeditions which were such an important dimension to education.

In the Higher Physics and Chemistry class we had to sit a practical and written examination. My practical test was to find the molecular weight of oxygen - wasn't I lucky I proved it exactly 16 and going towards the inspector to "show off" my ability I was aware that Allan Cameron (boy captain and later a doctor) had beaten me to it. On hearing him being allotted another practical physics experiment I beat a quick retreat and learnt "pride comes before a fall" - however I was successful in gaining Higher Science.

My most vivid memory of the war was the announcement of V.E. day, May 8th 1945. We were assembled in the hall and round the gallery to listen to the

The school's first ever group of prefects - Back - Andrew MacLaren, John Hill, Deverell Neill, James MacPhee. Middle - Allan Cook, Evelyn Cameron, Eiona Moir, Irene Stewart, Marjorie MacVinish, Simon MacMillan. Front - Mary Wylie, Callum MacAulay, D.J. MacDonald, Margaret Stewart, James Cattell, Isobel MacKay.

old radiogram which was wheeled into the hall. (This was actually May 7th - V.E. day being celebrated by a holiday on the 8th.) It was a very emotional occasion indeed with a few quiet tears shed. My brother was in Bomber Command and had flown on operations for nearly a year (almost a record). All I could feel was a wave of relief. In our own street, Telford Road, three of my brother's friends had been killed in the war. The Academy also had suffered many losses of former pupils, the young cream of our generation.

the 1940s

The Academy was almost certainly responsible for my choice of career. If a teacher was absent in the the sixth year girls were asked to take the class and so, despite Tommy Fraser's despair of "why not science", primary teaching it was."

Nancy went on to Moray House and from there straight into her first job at Inverness Central School. She retired after many years' distinguished service as Head Teacher at Smithton School.

In May 1944 D.J. introduced Prefects and Callum MacAulay and Margaret Stewart became the first elected School Captains. The following session the boy captain Craig MacIntosh and the girl vice captain Marjorie MacVinish both left before the end of the session. Jimmy Nairn stepped up to the top job with promotion to vice captain for Hamish Gray (later the government minister Lord Gray of Contin) and Chrissie Fraser.

Returning to the magazine, it introduced its comments on 1945 with an even greater ration of pomposity and pretension than usual, which really verges upon gibberish.

1946 appears to have been famous for an increase in the sweet ration, a greater flexibility of call-up regulations, an easing of the commitment to harvest potatoes and the introduction of the House system of Abertarff (blue), Dunain (green), Farr (red) and Raigmore (yellow). Meanwhile, the most memorable feature of 1947 was most certainly the severity of the winter, during which Mr. Galloway the janitor became a hero for the manner in which he kept the school warm.

In 1943, Dr. John MacLean became Director of Education for Inverness shire. Before long his son Ranald MacLean would

1945

The tremendous events that made an overwhelming background to our small domesticities, moved, through the year to their climax and consummation; and, in that August the background invaded the foreground, whence it is may hardly recede again, with the destruction, by human device of a few pounds of the substance of the universe, and, in its dissolution, of the Japanese cities of Hiroshima and Nagasaki. This was year one of the atomic era, of a significance to living kind on earth, not greatly less than the fabrication of the first living cells in the Azoic seas.

INVERNESS SWIMMING POOL AND BATHS
GLEBE STREET, BY RIVER BANK.

Superintendent—Mr P. M. MACGREGOR. Telephone—199.

HOURS OF BUSINESS

SWIMMING POOL

Monday to Friday, 9 a.m. to 8 p.m.

Wednesday, 9 a.m.—9 p.m.

Saturday, 9 a.m. to 6 p.m.

Sunday, 9 a.m. to 10 a.m.; 2 p.m. to 5 p.m.

Thursday (Ladies only), 6 p.m. to 8 p.m. Clubs, 8 to 9.30 p.m., Mondays, Tuesdays, Thursdays and Fridays.

PRIVATE BATHS

Monday to Friday, 9 a.m. to 9 p.m.; Saturday, 9 a.m. to 6 p.m.; Sunday, 8 a.m. to 12 Noon; 2 p.m. to 5 p.m.

Towels, Costumes, Bathing Caps, Soap, Pine Extract, Supplied.

The **Inverness Swimming Pool and Baths** were opened in July 1936, and have proved to be an increasingly attractive asset to the Town, not only from a health and sports point of view, but also as a Modern Social Amenity. No less than five Swimming Clubs are to-day being given facilities. The Pool is open as a rule for Mixed Bathing throughout the year, with certain exceptions, certain hours being allotted for Ladies only and for Clubs.

The Swimming Pool is one of the largest indoor Pools in Scotland, being 100 feet in length, 40 feet in breadth, and from 3 feet to 9 feet in depth. The Diving Equipment is Olympic Standard—1, 3, and 5 metres. There is ample Dressing Accommodation, together with Sprays, etc. The water is maintained at a temperature of 78°F. in Winter, and of 74°F. in Summer, the Building itself being comfortably warm in Winter, and in Summer, cooled by artificial ventilation. No effort is spared to ensure absolute purity of water at all times. This is effected by continuous filtration, ensuring a complete change every four hours or less.

There is a Modern Laundry on the premises to ensure an ample supply of Clean and Sterilised Linen and Bathing Costumes for all Patrons.

In addition to Swimming facilities, there are 15 First-Class **Private Baths**. There is a Waiting and Reading Room attached.

Foam Baths are also installed. This being a valuable remedial Bath for those suffering from Rheumatic Complaints and Obesity. It is also a fine Tonic Bath.

Qualified Swimming Instructors are available for Instructions to Swimmers and Non-Swimmers. Lessons by appointment. Under the Inverness Education Authority, Special Periods are reserved for the Swimming Instruction of the Burgh School Children.

CHARGES FOR ADMISSION.

SWIMMING POOL.		PRIVATE BATHS.	
Adults	6d	Admission	9d
Juveniles under 16 years	3d	Towels, Turkish	2d
Spectators—Adults	3d	Do. Honeycomb	1d
,, Juveniles	2d	Costumes	6d
		Bathing Hats	3d
		Bovril	3d per Cup

SEASON TICKETS.

| Adults | £1 5 0 | Half-year | £0 15 0 |
| Under 16 | 0 12 6 | Half-year | 0 7 6 |

Take the Plunge—Now!

1948 Magazine

become a pupil at the school before winning a scholarship at Fettes College, another stepping stone towards a legal career which saw him eventually become the eminent High Court Judge Lord MacLean.

However another FP, another early leaver too, went even further in the legal profession although his career had to take a political turn in order to do so. When Tony Blair's Labour government was returned in May 1997, one Derry Irvine was appointed Lord Chancellor and soon became famous for his exotic tastes in interior decoration.

Before long the media latched on to this colourful character. One of their first ports of call for information on the man who had been brought up in Dunain Road and Gordonville Road was his "alma mater". This was despite the fact that Irvine left at the age of nine, too young certainly to be able to blame Buckie's art classes for a liking for the visually sumptuous. Despite that, old school friends were traced and contacted and the family home filmed.

The following articles by the 9 year old MacLean and the 10 year old Irvine appear in themagazines of 1948 and 1949.

OTTER HUNTING

During the Easter holidays I had a good time. I was hunting otters along with Daddy and Iain, my friend We did not get one, though. Iain knows a great deal about it, and he told me a lot of things about the otter.

He is a carniverous animal and lives entirely on fish; being an excellent swimmer he is able to catch all the fish he needs-- that is about the otter, of course, not Iain. The otter resembles a dog, but it has much shorter legs. In a good season it can get very fat on all the fish it eats. It has a coat of smooth, waterproof fur, which is very valuable. To keep the skin whole the hunter traps it, but seldom shoots it.

On sunny days he comes ashore to eat his fish and lie out on the grass in the warmth, just like an old dog. His short legs make a track in the grass, and you can follow his footmarks in mud by the water's edge. They are sometimes rubbed out by his big tail. There is a song—"I found the wee brown otter's track."

RANALD MACLEAN (Form III. Lower).

AN ADVENTURE

It was a warm summer's day. A friend and I decided to spend the day in the country. So with lunch bags slung across our backs we set off gaily on our way.

We travelled many miles pleasantly but uneventfully. After a long stretch of barren country we came to a wood which looked cool and inviting. We decided that this was the very place to lunch.

We were just preparing to enjoy our lunch when a very quaintly-dressed man came rushing past us in the strangest manner. "A crook! fleeing from justice," we immediately thought and set off in hot pursuit. The quicker we ran, the quicker he seemed to escape us, as he dodged from tree to tree. We ran so far that we got entirely lost.

A few minutes later our crook came walking through the woods in a leisurely and no longer furtive manner. "Hello, boys," he said, "anything wrong?" When he heard our trouble he offered to take us to where we had left our lunch.

Our crook, we found out later, was a world-famous naturalist. When he ran past us he was chasing a rare butterfly to add to his collection. We arrived home after an exciting day, and—I hope, wiser boys!

DERRY IRVINE (Form IV), Junior.

Back - *Peggy Montgomery, Jean Douglas, Isobyl Bauchop, Isobel Brooman, Helen Ford, Alice MacLeod.*
Front - *Sandra Oliver, Aileen Munro, Peggy MacLeod, Miss Yule, Deirdre Munro, Vaila MacLeod, Margaret Oliver.*

"Up Stephen's Brae" contains a story which was acknowledged at the time as possibly apocryphal and which I now believe definitely to be so. This relates how Maude allegedly fused half the Crown area by short circuiting her low voltage supply. However it has now emerged that in 1946 some Second Year girls discovered a small electrical fire in the building which they reported to Miss Yule who took the necessary action. This is a long way short of plunging the area into darkness and is probably the reality on which the myth was founded.

the 1940s

Maude's other great contribution to school life was her coaching of the hockey teams and hockey balls, left out to dry after painting, were frequent sights in her room. Our photograph shows Maude with the 1949-50 1st XI. Sitting to the left of her in the picture is Peggy MacLeod from Raasay who herself went on to become a very well known coach and umpire in the sport.

Peggy's family connection with the school is far reaching. She married Andrew MacKintosh, the 1948 Howden Medallist and taught PE at Midmills for a time. Their son Callum also teaches PE at the school where he is Principal Teacher of Guidance. And his two sisters are gold medallists is entirely different disciplines. Rona was a member of the Royal Academy team which won the Scottish schools relay championship in 1977 while 21 years later Barbara won the coveted Gold Medal at the National Mod.

So ended the 1940s and as they gave way to the 50s, post war austerity gradually loosened its grip, difficult though that may be to believe, given some of the fashions of the next decade.

the 1950s

Bill Murray's appointment as head of PE in January 1951 - Festival of Britain year - marked a watershed in the school's sporting history. A specialist in rugby and athletics, Bill was soon to make extra curricular sport one of the major growth areas at Inverness Royal Academy.

This was a commitment which was to continue until Bill (pupils never referred to him as anything else among themselves) retired as an Assistant Rector in 1977. And in these early days D.J. MacDonald was more than content to encourage his enthusiasm and also to listen to his ideas which included the system of sports colours - half and full - which was soon introduced. In 1953, yellow braid was added to the royal blue blazers of both prefects and those with colours and it was not until 1969 that prefects were changed to silver to avoid confusion.

Early in Bill's tenure, in 1953, the 1st XV pulled off one of Royal Academy rugby's most famous results when they beat those longstanding rivals the Abbey 33-0 at Fort Augustus. In these days of three points for a try, there were seven - six from sprinter supreme Sandy Sanderson.

However Sanderson's personal high water mark that year came on the track when he won the Eric Liddell Memorial Trophy for the top performance at the Scottish Schoolboys' Championships at Goldenacre in Edinburgh. His time of 51.5 seconds for the 440 yards removed 0.6 seconds from the championship record and he was also in record breaking form at the SAAA championships where he improved to 50.6 seconds.

The school's outstanding girl athlete of the time was Annette Sinclair who at the Scottish schoolgirls' championships at Westerlands won both the 220 yards and the long jump.

There was a lot more to come from Bill's top athletes - particularly in the early 60s - but his interest also extended to grass roots level. Here in the early 50s he devised a system where each pupil was given a physical age group based on chronological age, but also significantly on weight and height. This avoided the injustice of the early developer sweeping the boards and gave everyone a chance.

Under this system a large first year could be found lining up to compete on level terms with an average second year and a small third year. It meant that all but the most obviously large senior pupils had to be measured annually, leading to a huge volume of calculation for Bill to place pupils in groups T,S,R,Q,P and O. But it led to the closest of competition at the school sports which became one of the most elaborate athletics meetings in the North.

Bill with the 1951-52 athletics team. Annette Sinclair and Sandy Sanderson are to the immediate left of Bill on the photograph.

Shinty flourished too. The 1954-55 shinty team with Curly. Back - Albert MacKay, Roderick MacIntosh, Dennis MacGillivray, Duncan Michael, Hugh Grant, Duncan Kennedy, Alan Stoddart Front - Alasdair Finlayson, Malcolm MacColl, Sinclair Graham, Peter English, Seumas MacInnes.

A description of an Inverness Royal Academy school sports is given on pages 89 - 91 of this book's predecessor "Up Stephen's Brae". But even in the pre-Bill days this was still a major occasion and extremely formal, with a large attendance of parents and friends. Latterly, girl prefects would provide the catering, but for much of the 1950s at least, this was franchised out to Burnetts the Bakers or the Balmoral Restaurant.

1952 saw the arrival of David Thom as Principal Teacher of Classics and a decade later he succeeded Pop Frewin as Second Master, a post he held until his death in harness in December 1970. Apart from his enormous contribution to the sport of cricket, David Thom was also well known as a frequently irascible starter at school sports and at other athletics meetings. Like W.S. MacDonald whose deputy he would become, David Thom had a great interest in the Boys' Brigade which at its peak had 12 companies in Inverness for a time.

In 1951 the bullet was at last bitten on a subject which in the late 1990s is fundamental to the PSE curriculum for both boys and girls and has even become a regular fixture in primary schools. On January 15th, in a characteristically complex sentence, reminiscent in its construction of Caesar's Gallic Wars, D.J. MacDonald recorded: "The Education Committee having decided to provide a course of talks for the girls of the Secondary Department in Sex Education, Miss Duncan, secretary of the Alliance of Honour, addressed a meeting of mothers in the Junior School hall at 7pm." He continued: "The Rector presided and Dr. J.A. MacLean, Director of Education, introduced Miss Duncan. Over 120 mothers were present. Tea was served by the Meals Department."

The objectives of the Alliance of Honour can only be guessed at, but right through to the 60s their Miss Annabelle Duncan provided lectures on what was later more normally referred to as "growing up".

The preliminary meeting of mothers (fathers were apparently never invited) was to be a common feature in the coming years, although later the lectures themselves were reduced to a couple of mornings and for Second Year only.

By the early 1950s the original 1895 part of the building was already over half a century old and dry rot had become a massive problem. Extensive operations to cure it began in January 1952 and at one point the floor of the hall was thick with dust and rubble, disrupting and on one occasion cancelling prayers. Dr. MacLean the Director of Education was called in at one point and appears to have made the fairly fundamental suggestion, which is probably nowadays enshrined in Health and Safety legislation, that the parts concerned should be boarded off. (How the top job has changed!) Even still, pupils had to be warned "to keep away from the area of work in the inner quadrangle for fear of falling masonry".

Almost 50 years after W.J. Watson expelled Lewis MacKenzie for

A happy group at the 1954 school dance.

frequenting ice cream parlours in Eastgate, the problem - which for decades was a Royal Academy institution - had got little better. In 1952 D.J. expelled one pupil and stripped another of his captaincy of the football team for nipping down town to play billiards during school hours.

the 1950s

In 1956 the heavy disciplinary hand also fell on the legendary Robbie Ewan who was deprived of the rugby captaincy. His offence was to have scaled the school tower and silenced the school bell by wrapping a rugby shirt round it. What he probably didn't realise was that 1956 was the bicentenary of the casting of that bell.

It was originally gifted to the old Grammar School in 1756 by one of its masters Hector Fraser, alias Hector Fraserius whose statue stood in Room 36, the old library, for years. The bell now stands in a case outside the Rector's office at Culduthel while Fraserius is in the library there.

Robbie Ewan, who eventually became secretary of Glasgow University and sadly died in post in his fifties, seems to have had some kind of campanological fixation because it as also he who around the same time claimed immortality by pinching the Gordonstoun bell. Rugby trips to Gordonstoun were regular occurrences and at that particular time relations between the two schools were at an all time low. In particular the Academy party were regularly made to feel rather less than welcome and something of an inconvenience at the school which was still half a dozen years short of receiving its most famous pupil.

So it was possibly as a result of what the young Ewan felt was less than courteous treatment that he surreptitiously removed a handbell from the premises. The Gordonstoun bell - known there as the Rioting Bell - was unobtrusively placed under Ewan's jacket as the 1st XV left the establishment after a particularly Soviet reception. Over the next few months, under the direction of Buckie in the Art Department, the Gordonstoun bell was given a plinth, painted in Royal Academy blue and gold and eventually given to Bill.

It received pride of place in the hallway of his home after he retired and it was only during the preparation of this book that he told me that the bell was also used to mark the final lap of mile and half mile races on Sports Day. Almost 30 years on, I learned that it was the Gordonstoun bell that sent me on the last lap of Royal Academy track titles in 1970 and 1971.

The next time anybody connected with Gordonstoun ever saw the bell was during the Bicentenary celebrations of 1992 when the then Rector Ian Fraser had to explain its presence in the historical exhibition to the visiting Prince Andrew.

It is at this point that I have to acknowledge the contribution of Buckie - or

the 1950s

to those who did not know him, Mr. Charles J. Buchanan of the Art Department and for many years Bill's partner in the rugby club. In a lengthy letter which he wrote to me after he had read 'Up Stephen's Brae' he elaborated on both Robbie Ewan 'bell' stories.

In 'Up Stephen's Brae' I quoted a story I had been told of a girl in the 70s who allegedly scaled the tower and did exactly the same as Ewan did in 1956. At that time I did not know the Ewan story, which Buckie told me in his letter and Bill Murray later confirmed in every detail. As a result I am now intrigued as to whether the girl's exploit was genuine or whether the story is an apocryphal version of Ewan's exploit.

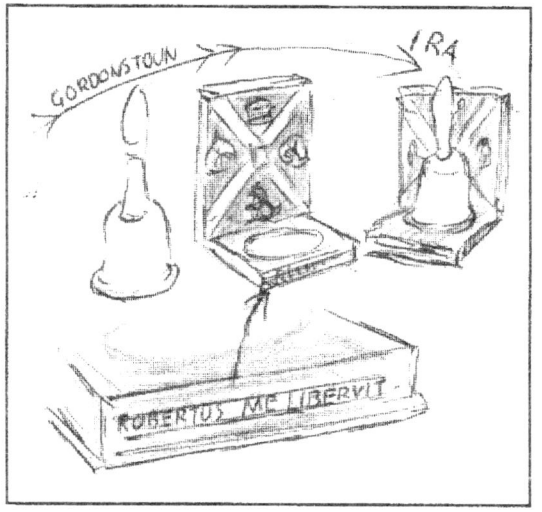

Buckie also went into detail in his 1995 letter about the Gordonstoun bell exploit and - almost 40 years on and at the age of 85 - provided a perfect sketch of it on its plinth with its inscription "*Robertus me liberavit*" - Robert freed (stole?!) me.

There appear to have been a number of rebellious spirits in the school in the mid 50s and in September 1956, D.J. MacDonald records: "In Tuesday's 'Courier' a false advertisement for an assistant janitor for the Academy brought about 70 men to the school. Investigations have now shown that the advertisement was given over the telephone......"

> ASSISTANT Janitor wanted for Inverness Royal Academy, £600 per annum. Apply in person between 2-4 p.m. at School Office.

A few days later D.J. "arraigned" two senior pupils at Prayers and "told the school that I had almost expelled them but decided to leave them in school on probation and out of consideration for the press and the publicity which their parents suffered since the bogus advertisement appeared."

D.J.'s 'presence' was never more evident than at Prayers and such is the recollection, extracted from the 1993 bicentenary historical folio but originating from the early 1950s, of Brian Denoon whose mother's memories of the 1920s have already been so vividly recounted.

D.J. conducting "prayers" - exactly as described by Brian Denoon

"Assembly was held every morning in the main hall. The whole school was present on these occasions. Most sat on low benches in the body of the hall; many others stood on the main stairway at the far end. Staff sat at strategic points around the periphery, and all were reasonably well catered for except a wretched couple of small groups of first year boys who, because there was no room for them anywhere else, had to stand at the radiators at the two points directly to the left and to the right of the Rector as he looked down from his raised podium and lectern.

The ritual of thse occasions had the whole gathering awaiting the moment when a dark curtain behind the podium was parted by an invisible prefect, allowing the magisterial figure of the Rector to climb slowly into view. It was all brilliantly stage managed. It was his custom, when he had reached the lectern, to grasp it in firm hands and to let his gaze reach out over the gathered

the 1950s

school, then to look down, imperiously, at the two huddles groups of first year boys immediately below him to his left and his right.

Now, all who passed through that school during the period of D.J's stewardship will testify to his immense presence: he was indeed a giant among educationalists. The following episode might thus be more readily appreciated. It is certainly etched upon my memory. On this morning, he had just climbed the steps, and the customary ensuing silence had fallen. His eye had, as usual, swept to the right and then swung in the direction of my group at our radiator. There came a sudden gasping sound and a heavy thud from directly behind me. One of our company of outcasts had fainted clean away and was now lying inert on the floor. He was duly gathered up and swept from sight, and assembly continued.

An incident like that didn't do much to ease the quaking nerves of a country misfit such as I. To me it announced that the rectorial eye had the power to fell a first year boy at twenty paces."

D.J. could be a disciplinarian when we wanted, but early in 1953 he issued an edict which was perhaps just a few years ahead of its time. He records on January 13th: "At a staff meeting held this afternoon I announced that pupils must not be struck on the head and that girls in the Secondary Department must not be strapped. Girls are not strapped in the Primary Department."

All the same a whack, or in Room 16 a knuckle, on the side of the head was still by no means unknown in the early 70s. And the belting of girls, albeit by a woman teacher and often a senior one, certainly took place in Scottish education right up to the abolition of corporal punishment in the 1980s.

However there is no record of the punishment meted out to the boy who stuck a pin in a First Year pupil's potatoes at school dinners one Friday in 1957. The pin was inadvertently swallowed and located by X-ray when Alec Munro the janitor took the lad to the RNI. The victim was back in school on the Monday, but D.J. records that there was no record of his having "lost" the pin.

In 1958 and 1959 there seems to have been a spate of burglaries at Midmills although it is not clear by whom. Among the items stolen on one occasion were a French dictionary, Vice Captain Robert Lindsay's books and, from Room 20..... "a tawse".

In 1955, the Education Committee, apparently to create more space for Secondary education at the school, decided to close the Royal Academy Primary Department on a progressive basis. There would be no further new intake and classes would disappear annually from the bottom up, ending the Primary Department by 1961.

This must have created much dismay at the time because this was an Inverness institution which was about to disappear. But although an integral part of the school for decades, it was also a relic of a fee paying era of privilege.

As the Primary classes steadily disappeared from the bottom, so did their teachers. In 1956 it was the turn of Infant Mistress Kate MacLean to be transferred to a similar post at Dalneigh School. It was there in 1958 that she gave me my very first experience of the education system when she enrolled me into primary 1. I have no doubt that the Royal Academy infants were just as much in awe of her as we were.

Academic selection in Primary 7 after the war, and right through to its abolition in Inverness in 1970, was done by the Promotion Examination and Intelligence Test, effectively the Eleven Plus. Each February, Primary 7 pupils all over the town and the surrounding area were shepherded into their various school halls and general purposes rooms. There they were confronted with these exams which, although they may not have fully appreciated the fact at the time, would decide their educational future.

Apart from the intelligence test there were exams in English and Maths. Most schools rehearsed their pupils intensively using past papers. An arithmetic paper was certainly a weekly ritual on a Friday morning at Dalneigh in the 60s and I have a clear recollection of the 1953 paper as a particularly straightforward one.

A high pass meant an Academic course at the Royal Academy while a lesser performance meant for boys a Technical course and for Girls a Commercial course at the High School. (There seemed to be some assumption that office secretaries would all be girls of the middle ability range.) For the rest it was a General course at the High School or, for those living east of the River Ness after 1961, at the new Millburn Junior Secondary. Even after that there was further hierarchical sub division within each course. In the Academy, where each and every pupil's IQ score was logged on an individual reference card, it was a case of 1A, B or C and latterly when numbers required it, 1D.

At one point in the mid 50s, D.J. recorded with some satisfaction that 90% of his own Primary 7 - some 24 pupils - had gained Academic courses and would be moving into the Secondary Department. Three would be going to the High School - one to a Technical course and two to General. This compared with the going rate elsewhere possibly of around 20% gaining entry to the Academy although it is difficult to determine a precise figure because the percentage grew along with the size of the Secondary Department.

But although, as many HMI reports have confirmed, teaching in the Royal Academy primary Department was no doubt excellent, this was not a level

the 1950s playing field. Indeed we have almost a preview here of the scenario which emerged early in the 1990s with the publication of League Tables where it was realised quite soon that one of the main factors related to educational success is affluence. And that was one thing of which there was no shortage in the Royal Academy Primary Department where the pupils came predominantly from prosperous, professional, middle class backgrounds.

The progressive disappearance of the Primary Department during the 50s released accommodation in that particular wing of the school which could be diverted to other purposes. Over this period it underwent a transition from Primary wing to the girls' wing. The roll at this time was around 220 in the Primary Department while the Secondary had 550 - a figure which was almost to double in rather less than two decades.

The primary assembly hall became a girls' gym and although the class next door to it briefly became Miss Forbes' maths room, its longer term fate was a changing room. Another class was divided in two to house the girl prefects and the Lady Superintendent while across the corridor a cookery room was created.

There were also girls' toilets in an era where many such facilities were still outdoors and were regularly out of action due to freezing - particularly during the icy winter of 1955. Frequently under these circumstances there would be enormous pressure on the unfrozen facilities.

A link with the past was restored in November 1956 with the unveiling of the Cockburn Memorial Library, a collection of over 700 volumes in three oak book cases. This was to mark the contribution to the school of a former teacher Thomas Cockburn who had died in 1947 at the age of 95 and who had served on the staff for 25 years. Contributions towards the cost had been received from all over the world from Mr. Cockburn's former pupils and the opening ceremony was performed by Dr. Evan Barron.

A year later there was a further gift to the school. In 1957 the Rector was awarded the honorary degree of Doctor of Laws by Aberdeen University and thus became "Dr. D.J." The honour was very well received indeed throughout the Royal Academy and in September of that year, to mark the occasion, the staff presented the school with a lectern bible which became a central feature of assemblies in the years to come.

Two of Dr. Macdonald's longest serving colleagues had their part to play too for the presentation was made by Tom Fraser, head of science, and the volume was inscribed by "Jake" Johnston, head of art.

However the presentation which dwarfed all others in the 1950s was that of the War Memorial gates in 1954. Yet another gift of the Old Boys' club,

OLD BOYS' CLUB NOTES

An ambition long cherished by the Old Boys' Club was fulfilled on Wednesday, 24th November 1954, when the Memorial Gates at the main entrance to the school were dedicated and handed over to the keeping of the County Council, and by them to the Rector on behalf of the school. By kind permission of the "Inverness Courier" we quote in full an account of the ceremony which appeared in that newspaper on Friday, 26th November.

"At a simple but moving ceremony in the Hall of Inverness Royal Academy on Wednesday afternoon, memorial gates, erected at the main entrance to the school by the Academy Old Boys' Club as a memorial to former pupils who died on service in the Second World War, were solemnly dedicated. The gates, which are twin-leaved, are made of wrought iron, and are of handsome ornamental design in the tradition of wrought iron craftsmanship. Each gate bears a fine reproduction of the Academy coat-of-arms.

Owing to the wet weather on Wednesday the dedication ceremony was held in the Hall, and it was attended by the pupils, rector and staff of the Academy, the school managers, members and officials of the Inverness Education Sub-Committee and of Inverness County Education Committee, and relatives of the fallen and others. Rev. A. A. Hamilton, B.D., St Stephen's Church, who presided, and Rev. G. R. Gilchrist, B.D., Ness Bank Church, the Academy Chaplains, conducted the religious service, which began with the singing of "O God our help in ages past," and a prayer by Mr Hamilton. Prior to the dedication ceremony, Mrs Bethune, wife of Dr W. J. Bethune, president of the Old Boys' Club, had cut the ribbon of Academy colours, blue and gold, which was stretched across the gates, and had opened the gates.

these were erected at the front of the school, immediately opposite the front door. This meant that access to it and to the entire school could now be gained by means of a single flight of steps up from the new gates while the old ones at each front corner were dispensed with.

The War Memorial gates marked the sacrifice of the 64 old boys who laid down their lives in World War II and their opening was prominently recorded in the 1954 school magazine.

To remember them within the building itself, Buckie designed and inscribed memorial panels which were hung - and still hang - beside the World War 1 memorial tablet.

During the 1950s the musical side of the school under Lawrence "Boosey" Rogers was as active as ever. The Christmas concert was an established end of term highlight and there were plenty of opportunities for aspiring singers and instrumentalists. Frequently items of equipment such as a radiogram, a record player and a new piano were acquired - largely out of the extremely healthy Endowment Fund. Drama also flourished.

Pupils also had many opportunities to attend performances outwith the school at places like the Arts Centre in Farraline Park and the Empire Theatre in Academy Street. The Empire was regularly the venue for Scottish National Orchestra concerts which were frequently attended by most of the school. The

the 1950s journey was inevitably by means of the famous Academy "crocodile" and there was a similar march to Prizegivings which took place at the Empire and, from 1955, the Playhouse Cinema. When that burned down in the early 70s, the Prizegiving was transferred to the school hall, thus ending the era of the crocodile.

The demise of the Playhouse also put an end to at least two institutions. No longer would there be a cafe with Disney inspired Christmas decorations to delight local children, nor would the same venue host afternoon tea for members of Academy staff at the end of the school day.

The end of the 50s spawned what was for a long time the highlight of the school's cultural year. On August 28th 1959, Mr. Gammie, Miss Cuthbert, Janet Banks and Eddie Hutcheon left with a 28 strong party of pupils for three days at the Edinburgh Festival. There is no explanation as to why Fritz did not follow them until mid afternoon, but he may well simply have forgotten about the trip.

Christmas play 1954 Producers Miss Eva MacKenzie, Buckie and Miss Anne Cuthbert with the cast.

This was the beginning of many opportunities for senior pupils, also getting their first experience of staying in Halls of Residence, to sample the delights of the Usher Hall, the Tattoo, Leith Town Hall, the Assembly Hall....... and of course, Rose Street.

For many pupils for years to come the visit to the Edinburgh Festival would be a memorable start to a session which finished in traditional style with the annual crocodile down town for the Prizegiving.

1957 was typical. On June 20th D.J. recorded, with perfect familiarity with the third person plural of the perfect tense of a verb of the third conjugation: "I held the annual meeting of Heads of Dept. to discuss the Dux. Decided that this year's Dux will be Murray Chalmers, and that Winifred Elliott and John Garvey be Proxime Accesserunt."

On the 28th the Prizegiving took place in the Playhouse. Burgh Treasurer W.J. "Bobo" MacKay, in a few years time to become Provost MacKay, presided and the principal guests were Sir Hugh Watson, Deputy keeper of the Signet and Lady Watson.

On this occasion it was goodbye to another Sixth Year and also to several staff. Miss Kerin of the P.E. Department transferred to visiting Primary work prior to her retiral. Miss Gordon of the Music Department left to go to Glasgow while Miss Goodsir headed for New Zealand. It was Miss Treasurer's turn to move from the shrinking Primary Department. Just as Miss MacLean had gone to Dalneigh a year earlier, Miss Treasurer transferred to its new sister school at Hilton. Mr. Kerr, retired Headmaster of the High School, also ended a number of spells of supply teaching in the Maths Department.

But although the 1950s appear to have been vibrant and active both inside the classroom and out, one Royal Academy institution which seems to have hit upon bad times towards the end of the decade was the "Smokers' Union", as the 'club report' from the 1959 magazine (overleaf) shows:-

At the very end of the decade, session 1959 - 60 was to be the last for several more members of staff, some of whose involvement with the school stretched much farther back than the 50s.

Of these, Miss Taylor of the Science Department, known to the entire pupil population as "Parrot", had been there since 1921. This diminutive lady was legendary for her ferocity and was known to mount a box in order to gain sufficient height to belt some of her senior boy pupils.

Jeannie Cruickshank taught German from 1928 and went on to enjoy a very long retirement indeed. Alex MacAskill left to become Principal Teacher of Gaelic at the Nicolson Institute in Stornoway, Miss Josephine Chisholm

THE SMOKERS' UNION
Annual Report

The demolition of our premises last summer dealt the Union a severe blow. A grief-stricken Sixth, lashed by the elements, prophesied that the S.U. would never again stagger to its feet. They were wrong. Mr Mactaggart, on assuming the presidential mantle, rallied the scattered forces of nicotine, and the Union, only a shade, but nevertheless a living shade of its former glory, is now entrenched along the main fence by the sheds, within sight of the mouldering ruins of its former ancestral seat. *Sic transit gloria vitae.*

Yet a few events shine out to lighten the gloom of this black year. The first is our outstanding success at the N.S.S.A.N.W. (North of Scotland's Schools' Association of Nicotine Worshippers). This organisation, to which we are affiliated, called an emergency meeting in November to discuss the possible effects of smoking on athletic performance. Our Rugby representative quashed the chicken-hearted with an argument of scintillating brilliance. This year's 1st XV, he argued, contains fewer smokers than last year's. Yet their performance has deteriorated still further. Therefore, smoking has no effect on athletic performance.

Our philanthropic president, ever mindful of the needs of youth, has instituted a Butt-ends' Bank. This is solely for the benefit of needy juniors who have not yet sufficient funds to enable them to indulge freely. Collection of butt-ends is made at the end of interval by Mr Driver.

On March 25th, we held our annual Remembrance Day, to the sacred memory of all those in the past who have suffered for the Cause. As a gesture of sacrifice, the Inner Circle met in Room 13, at 11.10, to smoke a cigar, kindly donated by Mr Gardiner, a former president.

We note with satisfaction that the Brown Stain has engulfed yet another of the yellow-braided peace-makers. This is indeed and encouraging sign. We have passed the t.p. of the parabola of despondency and are now clawing off from the x-axis with the glad song on our lips, "*Vivat nicotinia! Vivant omnes fumantes!*"

— SECRETARY.

went to teach art in Oban and it was Miss Elizabeth MacLeod's turn to depart from the Primary Department as yet another class was phased out.

The other departure was that of Principal Teacher of Geography Frank Cunningham who in his 14 years had made a huge contribution to the school in so many ways. Apart from his quality as a head of department he also had a great interest in football and spent a lot of time coaching a number of successful teams, including North of Scotland cupwinning sides.

His name as also synonymous with the Outdoor Club which for so many years occupied such a prominent place in school life. In 1957 he had been part of the British Expedition to the North Andes and that experience was certainly passed on to the Outdoor Club who at the time performed many climbs in the Highlands as well as in the Lake District, Wales and Switzerland.

Frank Cunningham with a group of geographers

Such farewells at the end of June are annual occurrences in schools, and for those involved, the end of an era. But as the 1950s gave way to the Swinging 60s, the end of an era was also at hand for the physical make up of Inverness Royal Academy as another major structural change began to take shape.

the 1960s

The flavour of the Sixties, or the second half of the decade at any rate, has hopefully already been conveyed in this publication's predecessor "Up Stephen's Brae", so this chapter has to a large extent involved a search for fresh material to avoid duplication.

By the late 1950s, as the post war baby boom began to reach secondary school age, the combined Primary and Secondary roll had risen to almost 800 and the building was packed to capacity. Although the decision had been taken to phase out Primary education at Inverness Royal Academy by 1961, it was anticipated that an expanding Secondary Department alone would continue to put pressure on accommodation. In addition there were certain modern facilities which were still lacking despite the fact that this was one of the major schools in the North. So in 1958 - 59 work began on the fourth phase of the building. This was a two year project which also involved extensive changes in the existing structure and caused great disruption within the school.

At one point Eddie Hutcheon, then in his first year as an English teacher, found himself teaching one class in the front half of the old Assembly Hall outside D.J.'s office. Unfortunately the other half, partitioned only by hospital screens, was occupied by one of Boosey's music classes and the piano and the noise Boosey's pupils made conspired to make English teaching all but impossible.

On Boosey's piano there stood proudly a potted flower, diligently tended daily by Jess Thomson - until someone anonymously cut the top off it. Jess went berserk and headed straight for D.J.'s office. The next morning at Assembly, even the worship of God was preceded by a lengthy inquest into the fate of Jess's flower.

This extension, which cost the ratepayers of Inverness-shire £114,000, was formally opened in 1961, although it had gradually come into commission from January 1960 when the transverse corridor containing the Second Master's, Medical and men's staffrooms forming the fourth side of the Quad was taken possession of. When complete, it arguably comprised the most significant of the four extensions which were made to the original 1895 building. It was also radically different from the rest of the school which was stone built between 1895 and 1926 and thus very much in keeping with the rest of the Crown where the housing was also begun in the late 19th century.

Although this new wing did not seem out of place in its more antiquated surroundings it certainly benefited from the dramatic changes in educational architecture seen in post war school buildings. It had a harled exterior and the large windows, unlike the older rooms, were actually low enough to be seen out of. The feel of the interior was definitely "20th century".

The new accommodation, apart from providing space for much larger numbers, also created new opportunities. A completely novel concept at this highly academic institiution was a room specifically designed for technical subjects with woodwork and metalwork benches. This became the preserve of the school's first Technical teacher Allan Beattie who would famously remind wasteful pupils that "wood doesn't grow on trees, laddie!".

A huge new laboratory was dedicated specifically to Physics, now that the three scientific disciplines were well on their way towards enjoying separate existences. This particular room, number 21, is inextricably associated with Maude who occupied it for the entire 18 years that it was part of Inverness Royal Academy.

Four classrooms upstairs comprised the History and Geography departments - the former ruled over by Farquhar MacIntosh, Sandy Cameron then Andrew Fraser and the latter by Jimmy Johnstone followed by Robert Preece. This meant that MacIntosh, who before long left to become Rector at Portree before taking charge at the Royal High School, could now return from his exile in the Crown School annexe.

The new medical room would soon see queues of terrified youth, having already suffered innoculation against polio at Primary school, awaiting the equally painful BCG anti-TB jag. In 1967, in the wake of a scare originating from the school field, the entire school also received the tetanus innoculation.

A new dining hall, with its octagonal tables, also eliminated the need for feeding at the Crown School. But possibly the most conspicuous Royal Academy institution to disappear as a result of that new building was "Prayers" in the old hall at the front of the school. These were now to be succeeded by "Assembly" in the vast new hall which, if the screens to the dining area were opened and the stage fully occupied, could - at a tight pinch - seat the 1000 to which the roll would soon rise.

This vast new facility also revolutionised the sitting of examinations and opened up enormous opportunities in the field of stage productions, some of which had previously to be mounted on the steps at the end of the old assembly hall. Bizet's Carmen and Sheridan's School for Scandal are but two of the more famous offerings of the mid sixties.

There were also profound changes in the old building. In 1962, ground floor partitions were built, creating corridors on their outside to feed the classrooms which had previously opened directly into the old hall. They also defined on their inside a slightly reduced area which became a much more

The 1961 Extension

extensive library than had previously been sited in the front-facing room which now became 36 as a result of an major renumbering.

the 1960s

In 1959 the school also changed over from coal to oil fired heating. Apart from making the cellar beneath the boys' entrance on Midmills Road available as a Sixth Year Common Room, this must have saved Alec Munro the janitor a great deal of physical labour stoking the boilers. However the new oil fired system had several teething troubles.

Back in 1955 Alec had received some initial reduction of his task of keeping the school warm, for the log book records on December 12th that: "Ashes hoists have now been installed in the furnace chambers and the Janitor has a bin trolley to move the bins from the top of the hoist to the points where the scavengers empty them." Since these days, a multitude of rather more politically correct terms have been developed for the humble "scaffy".

It may have been a combination of the physical alterations to the building and the phasing out of the Primary Department which led many to think that the begininng of the 1960s marked a fundamental change in the character of the school. Those, like myself, who did not arrive until the middle of that decade when Inverness Royal Academy was a selective secondary, might be easily tempted into thinking that the major change came with the introduction of comprehensive education in the 1970s. But many of a slightly earlier generation regard the developments which came to a head around 1961 as equally fundamental. The magazine article overleaf was written by Janet Lawson, one of the very last Primary pupils and a well known cartoonist as well, as she prepared to leave sixth year in 1967.

Viewed over the timescale of the quarter century 1954-79, changes to the school are even more profound. In 1954, Inverness Royal Academy still had seven primary classes numbering around 200 and six secondary years totalling over 500. By the time the new extension opened in 1961, the school had just become Secondary only, but numbering around 900 - a figure which was to reach 1000 by the end of the decade.

Although the school was still purely selective, the greater numbers did at least allow a larger range of "promotion" candidates into first year. Then by 1979, when Midmills was finally vacated, Inverness Royal Academy was fully comprehensive apart from a very last Sixth Year selected from Millburn at the end of S2 on the basis of doing at least one Higher.

But to return to the 60s, the new extension had not been open for many months when D.J. dropped the bombshell that he was to stand down early in 1962. He was just 61 and could easily have carried on for another three and a

Sic in Transit

This week I shall be leaving school, and, with any luck, without being expelled. I cannot truthfully say I am sorry to do so, but I must also admit a slight pang of nostalgia. This may seem ironic as I avoid being in school as often as possible. Nevertheless that establishment so honourably named the Inverness Royal Academy holds many memories for me, some of which do not bear repeating here.

Being in the school thirteen years I have seen several changes. We were the last class in the junior Academy - they felt there couldn't be another class after us! In the days of the "Caddie Rats" the school was rather different. The girls' gym was then the junior assembly hall and gym. Here in the mornings we had prayers which were a very solemn affair. Everyone had to clasp their hands and bow their heads (not, as someone said at school dinners, close your eyes and bow your heads). Prayers were usually conducted by Miss Grant, the headmistress, but occasionally by Dr D. J. MacDonald, the Rector, or Mr Frewin, the second master. We always knew when "Pop" Frewin was coming by the squeak of his shoes as he came down the corridor. Once I was reprimanded for keeping my eyes open, but I could never understand how the teacher concerned could see that my eyes were open when hers were closed.

Christmas parties were also held in the hall. The climax of these was Santa Claus' visit and the distribution of sweets and presents.

Of the hall as gym, my memories are of dusty bean bags, wooden hoops, whistles with peas that got stuck, and a ridiculous radio programme, like "Music and Movement."

On either side of the corridor, now the girls' wing were the primary classrooms, with high windows, not to be looked out of, and old much-carved, double desks with ink-wells. The girls' toilets were formerly the junior school staffroom, which was pretty stark and old-fashioned in contrast to the plush woman's staffroom which was once the girls' cloakroom and a classroom. The boys' cloakroom was at the other end of the corridor, and strictly out of bounds.

Recently, we have complained about the toilets in school which have minor defects such as no locks. However, the present ones are very luxurious compared to the ones in those days, which were outside, had no locks, paper, or seats, which rarely flushed in summer, and were frozen in winter.

The new building was not then in existence. The paved court a tarmac area, and the new block green fields and pastures. The playground really was a playground then. There were excellent muddy puddles for paddling in or sailing boats, long grass for hiding in or for making grass trip-ups on which no one ever tripped, and there was still room for a very active Smokers' Union to grace the playground. At the far end of the playground there was an old air-raid shelter which had various uses. Those of us who complain of school dinners should have sampled them about nine years ago when the menu was depressingly predictable and utterly indigestible. There was Irish stew which no Irishman would eat, a kind of mince (very runny) which you prayed would run off the plate, and cold beef or mutton with beetroot. Fish dishes consisted of rolled fish which was universally hated, fish pie made of bones in a paste, and baked fish in breadcrumbs. Peas were used for firing at neighbours. Dishwater soup was served once a week with black bread . At one stage, in despair we took to emptying our plates on to the floor when teacher's attention was elsewhere. The pig-bucket was generally very full.

When building on the new block commenced we were moved to the annex in the Crown School playground. Here we spent two isolated years in green corrugated sheds till at the end of Primary Seven we went to the "big school." For six further years I battled against books, teachers and fellows in the Senior Academy. In these six years there have been fewer changes in staff, clubs, societies, regulations and traditions.

In the seventies, schools go comprehensive and the Academy, as we know it, will vanish. At one time this would have been a big change, but as the school has already lost a great deal of its identity, tradition and reputation, perhaps the break will be less drastic. In a way I'm glad I knew the school when I did, but I have known it too long already. Good-bye, Academy

JANET LAWSON. VIa (M).

The last Primary 7 class with Miss Sinclair in 1961.

half years, but the man who had presonified Inverness Royal Academy for almost two decades was set to depart. A year or so previously Mrs. MacDonald had died and the loss of her support was almost certainly a factor in his decision.

His successor was another of the same clan, W.S. MacDonald, a native of Caithness who had a distinguished war record both as a corvette commander and as an interrogator of POW. He was an ex-amateur football internationalist who had honours degrees in three subjects, History, French and German from two universities, Edinburgh and London. As well as his degrees he had an MBE and a DSC to his name and had come to Inverness from Campbeltown Grammar with the highest of credentials. However he had the hardest of acts to follow in succeeding Dr. D.J.

The following is one day's entry from an imaginary third year pupil's diary, sometime during the 60s.

8:56 am... at least I hope it isn't any later than that because as I ascend Stephen's Brae I can hear the bell ringing out from the tower and if I get a move on, I may just be in time for assembly. As I sprint into the school and along the boys' gym corridor, Hairy Hugh bellows at me to stop running. He looks extremely red in the face and ready to explode.

8:59-and-a-half. I dash into assembly and collapse into a seat. Outside, a Hillman Minx is careering towards the plate glass window. The driver slams

the 1960s

on the brakes and screeches to a halt six inches short of the window. The first years on the inside seem used to this method of parking that particular vehicle - apart from the new girl who dives for cover under her seat. Maude locks the car, waves bye bye to the two Scotties abandoned on the back seat and enters the hall which is the usual cue for the bell to announce the entry of the Rector.

9:10 - End of assembly - we head for Geography in Room 34, aiming sly kicks at the prefects stationed along the middle of the hall corridor. Abdul is not in the best of form this morning and five minutes into the period takes Tommy outside to belt him. You could hear the screaming from inside the classroom........ but Tommy manages to suffer it in silence.

Periods 2 and 3 - (9:50 - 11:10) Double French with Curly in Room 16. However I have a clarinet lesson with Fred Short Period 2 and get the usual Spanish Inquisition from Curly when I go to ask off. Fred is sure my clarinet is leaking and lights up a Capstan Extra Strong so he can blow smoke down the barrel to check for a hole (or so he says.) As usual he finds nothing. At 10:30 I rush into Room 16 for the second period of French, to be met full in the chest by Curly's outstretched fist. Getting back into the class is nearly as difficult as getting out. On the board, Curluck has written up the answer to the ink exercise the rest handed in at the start of the period so I unobtrusively sort all my mistakes before I hand mine in. He marks it on the spot - and gives his own answer 16 out of 20! The only other damage is four hefty knocks on the side of the head just before the bell for forgetting the past historic of the verb "connaitre".

11:10 - 11:25 - Interval. We make our way out to the quad for our daily free milk. A third of a pint isn't much when you're trying to get rid of the taste of fag smoke after the clarinet episode, so I grab three. Oddjob shouts at me for being greedy.

Period 4 - (11:25 - 12:05) - Maths with Ma Hardie in Room 3. Stopped by Jess as we try to break the traffic regulations and go the wrong way round the library. She also sends the guy behind us packing - doesn't appear to realise he's the student teacher in the English Department who can go whatever way he likes. Maths is quadratic equations - boring!! Ma (4 ft 10) makes a token attempt to belt Billy (6 ft 2).

Period 5 (12:05 - 12:45) - English with Fritz in Room 7. He doesn't turn up until 12:25 - he thought he had a free period and had to be summoned from the staff room by the jannie whose suspicions were aroused when he spotted Harry out on the fire escape. When Fritz arrives, he thinks we are 5B and starts on Macbeth Act 2 Scene 3 while we (3C) have our books open at Julius Caesar Act 4 Scene 1. Fritz smells a rat when he realises Brutus is not one of the three witches.

Lunch (12:45 - 2:00) Just our luck to have the longest journey in the school from Room 7 to the dining hall. But it's 1st, 2nd and 3rd year at the front of the queue this week, so thanks to a combination of hard running and breaking several traffic regulations, we just get into First Sitting. However I am too late to get any of the serving spoons and so get tiny helpings of everything. After lunch, Hughie wants to buy a single out of Frankie Jew's so we head for Hill Street. Hughie pays Frank the threepence for the single, but I have to lend him the extra ha'penny for the match. We go up one of the lanes in front of the school so Hughie can smoke his fag while I eat my Five Boys.

Periods 6 and 7 (2:00 - 3:20) - Double Field - the usual parade, with bikes, down Abertarff Road, Crown Drive and Victoria Drive. Shock, horror!! Bill is away at a meeting and we've got Baillie! "Cross country today," he grins with that evil, sadistic sneer which tells us he won't be happy until we're all lying sick along the route. Somebody remembers how Baillie left three sixth year boys hanging from the wallbars for half an hour last term, and this doesn't help. Twice round the field, twice up Millburn hill, twice more round the field and we're all very happy to get back to the school, even if it is for Latin.

Period 8 (3:20 - 4:00) - Davie Thom in Room 14. It should have been Caesar's Gallic Wars but he spends most of the period telling us how British forces overran that particular area of northern France in 1944. And this is a mere prelude to his account of his personal contribution to Adolf Hitler's downfall.

4 pm - Round to Frankie Jew's for a Frosty Fingers and then down town for a Coke in the Cafe George. Still have 6s 8d left so round into the market to buy a copy of the Beatles' 'Strawberry Fields' from Bruce Miller's. On arriving home, read over sixty pages of Maude's notes for Physics test tomorrow."

The school magazines of the 1960s and 70s record in particular detail on their introductory pages the main events of the sessions which they brought to a close. The 1963 magazine, for instance, tells us that pupils returned for the new session in August 1962 to see the widening of the back stairway which joined Maths rooms 2 and 11. It was perhaps this physical link which in amphibious nickname parlance decreed that the occupant of the room above that of "Froggy" should be Christened "Toady".

On the subject of nicknames, I said in "Up Stephen's Brae" that no one really knew why Ian MacLean of the Physics Department came to be called Fred. Archie Fraser, the school's Principal Teacher of Biology since 1973 and a pupil during the early 60s, has since explained that this was because of Fred's close physical resemblance to the main character in The Flintstones.

the 1960s

Returning to session 1962-63, the school made its Top of the Form debut on radio (it still had not evolved into the television programme in which a team featured in 1970) in September 1962. Our photograph shows (left to right) the team comprising Penelope Wilson (S6), Joan Ford (S3), Fiona MacWilliam and Barbara Walker (both S2) along with W.S. MacDonald who had still not abandoned the mortar board. They beat a team of boys from Madras College in St. Andrews in the first round but unfortunately went out to Stirling High at the next stage.

Top of the Form Team

Also in September 1962, "Pop" Frewin retired as Second Master and was presented with the rather incongruous array of a suitcase, an electric toaster and a pressure cooker. On the other hand in the presentation repertoire of the early 60s, these were probably the equivalent of the modern day microwave or video camera. David Thom succeeded him as Second Master until 1970 while Allan Wilson became Principal Teacher of Maths until he retired in 1987.

Apparently the "ski boom" was under way in Scotland in the early 60s and there would have been no shortage of snow during the harsh winter of 62-63. The result was weekly Saturday trips to Cairngorm which became a longstanding institution, albeit less frequent in the milder climate of the late 80s and 90s.

On the social side, in December 1962 "Thirty or so bashful males invaded the almost cloisterally female precincts in Muirfield Road to make the Hedgefield 'At Home' the rousing success it always is." Of the two school dances on December 17th and 18th, the writer records, in that obscure and erudite style which is so typical of magazines prior to the 70s, that "a jarring note in the generally convivial atmosphere was struck by the not unreasonable attitude adopted to those precocious youngsters who partook of the spirit of the season 'not wisely but too well'."

One of the problems magazines have in their sports coverage is that summer events are still underway when they go to print and as a result there is scant reference to the marvellous achievements of the 1963 athletics season. The early 60s, like the early 50s, was a golden era for Bill's athletes who carried all before them at both local and national levels.

Jimmy Grant, school captain in 1962-63, was regarded by Bill as the greatest track athlete of his 26 years at the school. Jimmy, who gave up athletics when he left school for the Royal Dick Vet College, won four consecutive Scottish Schools 440 yard titles, breaking records in all three age groups. On his final British Schools International appearance in 1963 at Meadowbank, where he was also Scottish captain, he came so close to winning his event and it was to be another 36 years before an Inverness Royal Academy athlete finally achieved that distinction. Eddie Sharp could putt a mean shot, but was also quick enough to team up with Grant and two others in one of the finest relay teams ever seen at the Scottish School Championships which ran away with the title in 1962.

From the same year group, Miss Buchan's girls' hockey captain was Angie Urquhart who later married Alastair Hamilton who joined the P.E. Department in 1967. "Chunky" became Principal Teacher in 1973 when Bill became an Assistant Rector and left to become head of P.E. at the English School in Brussells in 1991.

A couple of years below that was Tom McCook who in 1965 brought the School Sports record for the mile to within an ace of 4 minutes 30 seconds. When Tom moved to Birmingham with the Post Office he married into a famous athletics family and became the brother-in-law of 1970 Commonwealth 5000m champion Ian Stewart.

Possibly the overwhelming event of session 1963-64 was the death, after only a very short period of retirement, of Ethel C. Forbes whose teaching of mathematics in Room 3 was as legendary as her role as Lady Superintendent.

Full page tributes from both W.S. and D.J. MacDonald, the contribution of the former a transcript of what he said at her memorial service in the Crown Church on May 29th, 1964, appear in the magazine. And although D.J. was the accepted master

1963 Hockey Team
Back : J Macrae, J Fraser, S Hamilton, Miss Buchan, C Fraser, D Gauld
Front : C Ross, M Cameron, A Urquhart (Captain), S Forbes, J Munro, P Finlay

of this and so many other communicative arts, his marvellous words are perhaps just edged into the shade by his successor who concluded: "In the long history of Inverness Royal Academy, she occupies and will always occupy an honoured place. All who have shared her friendship, all who have come under her influence, all of us here this morning, can say with sincerity - We were privileged to have known her. A gracious, vital, warm-hearted person has gone from our midst and we are the poorer for her passing. We are grateful for her life among us, we honour her memory."

This was also a time of rapid increase in staffing, with arrivals vastly outnumbering departures. In 1962-63, new recruits included Sandy Cameron (Principal Teacher of History), Douglas Kennedy and Alan Dougherty (English), Alison Buchan (P.E. and soon to become Mrs Seeley) and Ann Rose (Homecraft). The following session Dr. Charles Edward Stewart joined the Physics Department and retired around 30 years later as Highland Region's Director of Education. Also making their debuts in 62-63 were Barbara Spence (History), Sheena Osler (Classics) (one of the band of bright young things soon to be sporting beehive hairstyles) and Jim "Bonzo" MacKintosh (Geography).

In 64-65, eight new arrivals on the staff included Isolyn Urquhart in the English Department, Kenny Campbell in Modern Languages and Kate MacKenzie. At the end of that session Duggie ended her permanent employment in the Modern Languages Department to the customary valedictory in the magazine, but also to this rather less conventional farewell tribute:

> **OVERHEARD FROM ROOM 12 AS PUPIL ENTERS 5 MINUTES LATE**
>
> D'you realiiize you are **faive** minutes late. Iiii'm awl for a bit of fun but it is **tiime** we were getting down to some **Honest to Goodness!!! Down to Earth!!! Hard!!! Work???** Sit up Roberrr, do you rechoire an aarmchair? Melvinn! A little more ayer, plaize. Bi the **way** Renald, did you listen to the radio at **faive** to eight this mouning? It's **hiigh tiime** you made yourself **aliive** to the situation. D' you follow. (**Bi** the way, see me at the end of the period, Ian). The first year . . . or was it the sixth, had this werd this mauning — take it down and fiiind it for to-morrow."
>
> (Bell rings). Bleck**baud**, Roberrr. Now Ian . . .
>
> R. M. S., R. G. A. S., J. C. W. M., V.

This may also help readers of "Up Stephen's Brae" who had difficulty understanding the reference there to Duggie and Miss Jean Brodie probably having been flatmates in Edinburgh.

Among a number of pupil achievements that session were Elisabeth Caird's first place in the General Subjects section of the Edinburgh Bursary, the selection of George Stapleton for the Scottish Schools Football team against Wales and England and various academic successes by Stephen Walker who, as the magazine rather enigmatically puts it "as some of you may not have heard, won an extremely valuable B.P. scholarship."

Retired Chief Inspector of Schools Miss Edith Young (who, according to an anecdote of Eddie Hutcheon's, best not repeated here, may not have been one of Fritz's favourite people) handed over the awards at the 1964 Prizegiving. The Duces were Gordon L. Smith and Gordon Kennedy while the Howden Medals went to Shelagh Hamilton and Hugh MacDonald.

That October the 'mock election' mirrored the Inverness constituency result. Liberal candidate Douglas Sinclair matched the feat of the young Russell Johnston whose 33 years at Westminster began then and who in the run up to the real poll participated in a hustings at the school along with rivals Allan Campbell MacLean (Labour) and Col. Neil MacLean (Conservative).

PREFECTS – 1963 - 64

Back Row : George Stapleton, Anne Barton, Nicolas Ledingham, Helen Barlow, Neil Sharp, Barbara Pollitt, J. Stephen Walker, Jane Gray, Christine Ross, Calum Elder.
Front Row : Janet Fraser, John Latham, Ann Barlow, Hugh MacDonald, Shelagh Hamilton, Gordon Smith (Boy Captain), Mrs Anderson, Mr MacDonald, Sandra Marshall (Girl Captain), Andrew Morrison, Patricia Finlay, Hugh Cameron, Jennifer Gordon.

Ian Bowman returned in December 1964 after several months' absence as a result of a motor accident On January 29th a memorial service was held for the recently deceased Sir Winston Churchill. And that June, pupils were really on the move.

Douglas Kennedy took 140 to the Pitlochry Drama Festival while Jimmy Johnstone led a party to Switzerland. Meanwhile the Outdoor Club went to Northern Ireland while 25 years on from the surrender of the 51st Highland Division, a group went on an exchange visit to St. Valery en Caux.

The following article from the 1968 magazine helps to give a flavour of the school towards the end of the decade:-

Formula for Success

For success in life, you must follow the following formula:—

$$S = \frac{ms^2 - gh}{E}$$ where S is success in plenty.

R.11 makes you proficient at poetry. That is SOH, CAH, TOA. Honesty is achieved here. Return log tables, rulers, and instruments after the term exam. These valuables will be no use to you anyway... what... stamped with ASW?

If you are under instruction from R.13, watch you don't trip over rucksacks, climbing ropes or cuboids made with drinking straws. This develops smartness on your feet.

Murdo is a truly inspiring man. Sympathise with him while he tells you about the hard times he had when at university. You soon forget about the homework you forgot to do, and when he finds out, you're surely a fathead!

Physics with M.P.C. will mean many thousands of hand-written notes (which strengthen your wrist), and as many duplicated sheets. Learning Jardine No. 3 will set you in good stead for life! Distractions may come in the form of family news, but don't worry. Treat it all with interest, as it will make you drift from Ohm's into the family tree at 21. Relaxation from stress is the result.

Chemistry with the now emigrated tall chap, who loved stotting a ball in the gym, appeared stimulating until your equations no longer balanced. Patience was encouraged.

Hugh gives an assortment. For your money you can usually get some gardening, history and meteorology. Variety is the spice of life!

People with weak hearts must beware when his nibs the Bonzo crashes in yelling mild accusations of neglecting the work. But as long as you know the difference between a shuttlecock and igneous rock, you'll be a winner.

His neighbour is semi-detached. He enforces promptness, and if you're late, his bow tie almost lights up. But he comes out with the wittiest cracks. Joviality aids learnability.

The author-cum-historian breaks down kings to chaps, blokes and good fellas. His neighbour demands tidiness and gives severe punishment for drawing the Saint on desks. Even if you plead complete insanity, she still makes you paint the battle of Culloden, improving your hidden artistic talents.

The lass in R.37 develops culture. Shakespeare, Shelley, and even the aristocratic way to clear your throat.

When applying the formula, choose a calm day for your first attempts. Although S is a constant, msghE may vary. Good luck...

FRANK FALLER, V.

As far as the author can determine the teachers referred to (in order) must be Allan Wilson (Principal Teacher of Maths), Murdo MacDonald (Maths), Maude, Peter Higgins, the basketball fanatic who left the Chemistry Department to emigrate around 1967, (Hairy) Hugh MacDonald (Chemistry), "Bonzo" MacKintosh, Jimmy Johnstone, Principal Teacher of Geography who became Depute Rector on David Thom's death in December 1970 and retired in 1989, A.D. (Sandy) Cameron, who wrote the standard First and Second Year textbooks "History for Young Scots" and Isolyn Urquhart.

A reference in the 1969 magazine to the death of "Mr. R. Chisholm Assistant Janitor" must have caused a few heads to be scratched because few knew of him as anything other than "Oddjob", a title which equally defined his task in the school and his resemblance to the character in the Bond film Goldfinger. Many pupils from the 60s will have been ejected from the building to a roar of "Gerrout-SIDE".

Another of Maude's eccentricities was her obscure system of naming some pupils, which appeared to be loosely based on the Icelandic patronymic convention where you received your title from someone close to you.

As a result Stewie Donald, as was the case with all boys, was quite simply "Donald" and from that, all linked to him were defined. So when Stewie and his father bumped into Maude one day on holiday, they promptly received the greeting "Hello Donald and Donald's dad!"

It got worse. When Gillian Donald came to the school in 1968 and went into Maude's Physics class, she was never referred to as anything other than "Donald's sister." This also meant that the girl who sat beside her had to settle for "Donald's sister's friend."

The 1960s were in may ways a period of great stability at Inverness Royal Academy. They were also largely W.S. MacDonald's decade. The extension had been opened in 1961 and D.J. and the last of the Primary Department had gone very soon afterwards. From then until the retiral of W.S. in 1971, which also saw the start of the move towards a comprehensive system, very little changed. But when things did begin to move in the early 70s the changes which followed would be very profound indeed.

Caricature of Oddjob

the 1970s

There can be no decade which will be looked back on with more sartorial embarrassment than the 1970s. Many wearers of flares, platforms, tank tops and perms will be approaching middle age by now and will no doubt cringe at the excesses they displayed in their schooldays in the name of fashion.

During the 60s, W.S. MacDonald waged a constant war against long hair but towards the end of his tenure he eventually had to begin to concede defeat. The 70s were not very old when fringes began to creep relentlessly downwards, blossoming rapidly into the full blown, wavy perm which was so characteristic of the middle years of the decade. And that was just the boys! By the time Ian Fraser took over in 1971, change was well established with the Sounds of the Sixties well on their way towards being replaced by the Sights of the Seventies.

In certain ways, despite rolling change, the school which began this decade of Slade, Watergate, Ted Heath and the Wombles was not really all that different from the rather stuffy yet vibrant academic establishment which had existed at Midmills since the end of the previous century.

On the other hand, during no decade in 200 years of Inverness Royal Academy did educational change take place as rapidly as in the 1970s. The period began with the school as a fully selective establishment at the top of Stephen's Brae. It ended with full comprehensive status at Culduthel, the profound changes which took place having almost exactly encompassed the ten year period in question.

The First Year intake of 1970 was the last to be selected by the Promotion exam and indeed the last intake of any kind until 1973. At this point the pairing arrangement with Millburn Secondary School which lasted for four sessions began to feed pupils capable of doing Highers into third year. Then from 1977, after this brief episode as a four year senior secondary, the Royal Academy received its own fully comprehensive intake from its freshly defined catchment area of Hilton, Holm, Lochardil and the landward area bordering the east shore of Loch Ness. By the end of session 1979-80 the last pupils who had been fed in from Millburn departed to leave a fully comprehensive six year secondary school on the Culduthel site.

It must have been disconcerting for that last selective first year of 1970 to have had not one but three sessions as the youngest pupils in the school before the beginning of the pairing arrangement. Indeed the experience may even have created in two members of that year group a subconscious desire to help equally traumatised children by embarking upon careers in Guidance. Certainly it appears not to have prejudiced Donny MacLeod or Callum MacKintosh

What's New at Johnstone's?

Exciting new casual wear for the younger generation . . .

- ★ **SHIRTS** — by Go Man! - John Langford - Ben Sherman and Black Bear
- ★ **JACKETS** — by "Man Apparel" and "Male Mood"
- ★ **TROUSERS** — Slim Line - Parallel - or as Flared as you like

JEANS
in
Brushed
Denim,
Dune Buggy
and
Corduroy

All in the
new wide
flare

SHETLAND KNITWEAR

Polo neck
Crew neck
and the
new
U neck
by
"Macaul"
and
"Playfair"

Lee Cooper gives you a lot more style

See them at:

Wm. Johnstone
OUTFITTER
New Market Hall, Inverness
Telephone 35683

1970s - the decade of the flare.

against their old school where at the time of writing they hold the posts of Assistant Rector and Principal Teacher of Guidance respectively!

the 1970s

Apart from his prowess on the rugby field, Callum will also be remembered in his first year as the 'little drummer boy' in Richard Rodney Bennett's 'All the King's Men' which shared a double bill with Purcell's 'Dido and Aeneas' in June 1971.

Coincidentally, Donny's and Callum's current posts were two of the extra teacher grades which came in during their time as pupils at the school. A radical overhaul of promoted posts introduced Assistant Rectors and teachers of Guidance both at the Principal Teacher and the new Assistant Principal levels, the latter also also coming into larger subject departments.

Bill Murray and Sandy Cameron were the school's first Assistant Rectors, although the latter soon left teaching and was succeeded by Jim Sim, a move which opened the door for Jim Dunlop to become Principal Teacher of Chemistry for 20 years. The original Guidance staff were Torquil MacLeod and Ann Rose, previously Lady Superintendent, and they were soon followed by Margaret Murray and Jane Graham.

Because the youngest pupils at Midmills were for a number of years in third year the place was at least spared the worst excesses of the Bay City Rollers phenomenon which reached its "Bye Bye Baby" zenith in 1975. By the time 14 year olds were preparing to embark on "O" Grade courses at their new school, they were beginning to grow out of this particular craze of Woody, Les and the boys. But although Royal Academy pupils were not entirely exempt from sawn off jeans with tartan stripes and similarly adorned white shirts, there was something of an epidemic of the craze at Millburn with its 500 pupils in each of the first two years.

One other pop phenomenon of the 70s was the glut of memorable Christmas "No 1s" (or near misses) which probably reached their high water mark with Slade's "Merry Christmas Everybody". These gave those last few school dances at Midmills a particular flavour. But none of these events was quite as poignant as what was called "The Last Waltz" - the very final dance there in December 1978.

Most decades saw the departure of school legends and the 1970s were no exception. W.S. MacDonald himself demitted office in September 1971 to embark upon a hectically busy but tragically short retirement.

Soon after he left he began a post graduate course in Divinity and quickly became a fully fledged minister of the Church of Scotland. He and his wife Connie, who had done numerous periods of supply teaching in the Modern

the 1970s Languages department, moved back to their native Caithness. They set up home in the tiny village of Scarfskerry on the exposed North coast which offered him an unrestricted view of the sea which he loved so much. It was there that I went to see him in 1974 when I was looking for an independent opinion as to whether I should abandon my original plan of a PhD and enter teaching. The visit played a big part in my final decision and it was the last time I ever saw him.

Bill MacDonald's next step was to become the local member of the fledgling Highland Regional Council where he played a big part in the Education Committee in particular. However, hard on the heels of adjusting to the demands of a new profession and the politacal world of the Council, repeated journeys from the north coast to meetings in Inverness must have taken their toll and he died suddenly in January 1978.

Alan Findlay with the Outdoor club 1973-74.

W.S. MacDonald had a hard act to follow in D.J. and did so more than adequately. If anything he was perhaps, as Lady Macbeth said of her husband, "too full of the milk of human kindness". This at times generated a rather excessive faith in the fundamental goodness of human nature which, for instance, led him on one occasion to tick off the Janitor as the source of the smell of cigarette smoke in the Sixth Year boys' toilets!

In 1972, Jess Thomson ended what for her was, barring her distinguished time at university, a 60 year association with the school of which she had been dux in 1924.

Within the previous few years Tomuck had already gone, as had Fritz, Boosey and Duggie. Parrot's departure was already a rather distant memory and in 1973 it was the turn of Curly to stand down as Principal Teacher of Modern Languages, a post he had held for 20 years. In not much more than a decade, the substantial core of staff which had given the school so much of its unique character for over 30 years departed, but the Royal Academy survived with a continuing freshness.

Then in 1979, at a time when the school also ended its association with the Midmills building, Maude - the last and in many ways the greatest of the Worthies - ended her 40 year period of teaching Science and Physics at Inverness Royal Academy.

Culduthel was never really Maude's kind of place. For a start this comparatively large lady took not at all well to having to climb two flights of stairs to reach the Science Department on the top floor. And this was quarter of a century after a persistent knee problem had forced her to have the joint operated on. Also, after 40 years of teaching academic pupils in a selective environment, the thought of S1 and 2 mixed ability Integrated Science in accordance with Curriculum Paper 7 must have appalled her.

The retiral of Maude P.C. Anderson - her triple ambition of the car, the fur coat and the man long since achieved - confirmed the school's recently altered identity. It was strangely appropriate that the completion of the changes required to bring that about should have been accompanied by the departure of the last great worthy on the staff, the last human symbol of the era which had just concluded.

When W.S. MacDonald retired, it fell to Ian Fraser to take the school into the comprehensive era. A native of the Glasgow area, he had taught Geography for a time at Elgin Academy before becoming Rector of Waid Academy in Anstruther from which he was appointed to Inverness in 1971. Apart from implementing a number of administrative changes in the mid 70s, he was also responsible for the major task of planning, both educationally and logistically, for a move to comprehensive status at Culduthel.

His interests included rugby and in his earlier years he refereed a number of school matches. He clearly took the impartiality of a "home" referee very seriously because, in one school magazine interview, he records his mortification at replying, when asked for whom a penalty was being awarded, "for us".

However, the discontinuation in the early 70s of the practice of keeping a

the 1970s

log book deprives us of some of the flavour of Ian Fraser's years in charge.

One member of staff who saw a great deal of the profound changes which took place during the 1970s was Eddie Hutcheon who arrived as an Assistant Teacher of English in 1958, just as work on the new wing was beginning, and who became Principal Teacher in 1968 when Fritz retired. He was also very active on the football front where he ran the Junior XI for six years and the 1st XI for another thirteen and he gave almost 35 years to the school before retiring in 1992. Among his memories of the 70 are the events running up to comprehensive reorganisation, and the reaction that produced. The following are the highlights of a long conversation I had with the man who taught me English for all six years.

"There was a lot of feeling that the old Academy was going to go altogether. There was a committee formed to oppose a lot of the changes which were due to take place at the time and it had Russell Johnston's support and quite a lot of the staff were supporting it too. I didn't feel particularly strongly about it but some of the older teachers felt very strongly indeed - they thought that 'this was dreadful'. When pupils started coming up from Millburn, I can't remember it having any great effect on the standards within the Academy. The pupils we had then were more or less as we had had before.

W.S. MacDonald in his day used to stand and stop folk and tell them to get their hair cut although by the time the 70s came along hair had definitely got a lot longer and you can see that, for instance, in photographs of footballers. On the other hand there was no pronouncement about mini skirts in the 60s like there was against hair. Eventually, I think the older generation, if they were not prepared to accept longer hair, did accept that the battle was lost.

When the cleaners went on strike in 1976 they had support from the pupils and I think some came up from Millburn to join them in a demonstration but it was all peaceful. Probably a majority of teachers supported the cleaners as well. There were also teachers' strikes in the earlier 1970s and they caused a lot of ill feeling.

When Culduthel opened in 1977 I had Fifth and Sixth Year classes at Midmills as well as junior classes up there so that meant a lot of travelling. The timetables were staggered by 15 minutes and Pat Haughey, the Assistant Janitor used to spend much of his day ferrying staff between buildings. There was also a flitting in 1977 when we had to take a lot of books and equipment from Midmills up to Culduthel and when the building opened first I had a room in the ground floor in the main building although I was quite happy for the English Department to get the chance to move out to the huts when they came along after they decided not to go ahead with the planned second phase of the school

Back: Elaine Munro, Christine Ross, Jane Cumming, Jill Morgan, Miss Macdonnell
Front: Sheila Cameron, Caroline Mackinnon, Norma Elliot (captain), Helen Cattell, Wilma Brownlee

1977 basketball photo and 1974 cricket report

CRICKET

More matches can be reported on this year, but, on the debit side, there is no photograph of this year's Senior XI, which has only three regulars from last year — the captain, Hamish Dodds of V year; and Laurie Chancellor and Peter Nicholson from the remnants of the VI year. Five games have been played, only one resulting in defeat. This was the annual First - Wednesday - in - June fixture against the Abbey School. In the North Schools' competitions it is again Forres Academy that stands between our school and a place in the finals of both League and Cup. Our performance as a team was best shown against Northern Counties' 2nd XI — sharp fielding, accurate bowling and good running between wickets when batting. In the other games all three aspects have not clicked at the same time.

Mainstays of the team are Dodds and Chancellor, and new recruit Ronald MacKay of V has had some good performances. Peter Nicholson has shown improvement from last year, as has Eric Fraser of IV, who is also vice-captain. Both were at the coaching sessions run last winter. Callum MacIntosh, IV, and Alan Barrie, III, also attended sessions at R.A.F. Kinloss and will vie for the place of wicket-keeper next season. Barrie has already played for the Senior XI, also making a contribution with his batting. He captains the Junior XI in their games — a win against the Abbey, a defeat by Gordonstoun.

The Juniors are very enthusiastic and have had interest maintained throughout the winter by Mr Morrison's lunch-time coaching classes in the Gym. Even if the school trophies do not grace our showcase this coming session, it will not be long until they do so.

I took over the 1st XI in 1964 and that was a good side, captained as it w[...] by George Stapleton who was a regular in the Scottish Schools XI, as was t[...] 1969 team which returned for reunion matches with the school in '79, '89 ar[...] '94. Our 1st XI was invariably in the running for league and cup honour[...]

Back: Eddie Hutcheon, Bryan MacGregor, John MacQuarrie, John Mackenzie(Captain), Andrew Smith, Ian Harrower,
Front: Kenny Campbell, Billy Urquhart, Davie Milroy, Jeff MacDonald, James Jack, Norman MacSween

including the 1974 side which had Kenny Campbell on the right wing, And[...] Smith at inside right, Brian MacGregor, who was School Captain, at cent[...] half and Jeff MacDonald at left half. And of course in these days we had bot[...] Billy Urquhart and Davie Milroy up front. It wasn't until Willie Grant came [...] Inverness Thistle as manager that Davie became a defender which is how he [...] best remembered, but he scored a record number of goals as a striker in scho[...] teams.

We also had three enjoyable trips abroad to Germany and Holland in 197[...] 73 and 75 when my colleague from the English Department Ian Fraser, Ia[...] Thomson and Gordon Harvey came with me at different times."

In his sixth year Milroy scored 47 goals for the 1st X1, including eight hat tricks in nine games, bringing his total for Royal Academy teams to a record 214. However his longer term future was in defence and it was Urquhart who continued to play up front for Rangers and for Caley, giving rise to many great tussles in local derbies between the two former team mates. Urquhart ended his career as the oldest player ever to turn out in the Scottish League for Caledonian Thistle at 38 years 172 days in 1995.

the 1970s

It is unfortunate that the 1973 school magazine was the last to feature a month by month report on school activities, because in other decades these have given valuable insights into the life of the place.

September 1972 featured the Schools to University conference, the Geography field trip to Skye and an excursion to Aberdeen for head of Physics Jim Wilson and senior pupils for a course on new gadgets called computers. (As a reminder of how novel such technology was, one 1970 edition of the New Scientist carries an advert for one of the very first and very basic electronic calculators, at the stupendous price for the time of £70!)

In November, the Briitsh India line, owners of the 'Dunera' and the 'Uganda', gave an illustrated talk on school cruises while Tommy Docherty spoke to the footballers. The following month "Our own sixth year were joined by their counterparts from the High School in a race relations conference in the school hall." Were tensions between the two schools really as bad as that?

Into 1973, School Captains Kay Sutherland and Andrew Seal along with James Finlayson took part in the Inverness Speakers' Club competition while in May, Graham Lilley won five gold medals at the North District swimming championships.

During session 1976-77, schools in the Highlands suffered from a long running cleaners' strike to which Eddie referred. This meant filthy floors and large accumulations of rubbish in establishments all over the area. With the 'Winter of Discontent' on the horizon, this was the era, in advance of the constraints of Conservative industrial relations legislation, when Trade Union power was at its zenith and workers were wont to walk out at the drop of a hat. And the pupils of Inverness Royal Academy did not require much persuasion to become involved too.

When the strike was at its peak a large group of senior pupils staged their own walk out in sympathy with the cleaners which culminated in a noisy march round the school. This however did not go down at all well with local residents, particularly the occupants of one nearby house who had had a bereavement and became extremely annoyed at the disturbance.

the 70s 1979 By the mid 70s Inverness Royal Academy's days at the Midmills premises it had occupied since 1895 were well and truly numbered. Construction of the new building at Culduthel had begun with a view to it coming on stream in August 1977, quickly becoming the school's exclusive premises after a transitional split site arrangement.

From August 1977 onwards the scope of the Midmills building was further run down from the S3 - 6 it had accommodated for the previous five years to S4-6 in 1977-78 and S5-6 in 1978-79. At this point in the summer of 1979, Midmills was vacated in order to provide a temporary home for the fledgling Culloden Academy whose inaugural rector was to be Derek McGinn. This actually meant that some kind of connection perpetuated for a short time because Derek was himself an FP from the 1950s and was promoted to the job after a short spell as a Royal Academy Assistant Rector.

But to all effective intents and purposes, Inverness Royal Academy parted company with Midmills in June 1979. For those on the staff at the time there were varying degrees of sadness, which was probably at its most acute among longer serving members and FPs. But at the same time there was the incentive of everyone being on the same site once again up at Culduthel with the singularity of purpose associated with the six year comprehensive status which had finally been reached.

Perhaps those who least understood the move were those who were least involved - FPs furth of Inverness, some of whom were even outraged at what for them had been "school" being handed over initially to a sister establishment and then in the longer term being occupied by the Technical College.

I even had a letter from one FP in Australia who for years had believed that the school had actually disbanded at this point. He was delighted to discover from reading 'Up Stephen's Brae' that Inverness Royal Academy was alive and well at Culduthel.

It was this correspondent who told me of the rubber soled shoes which Fritz acquired for a time in the early 50s and which made such a loud squeaking sound that he could be heard coming from far enough off for riotous classes to descend into complete silence before he could make an entry. But that was not what made these shoes disappear as suddenly as they had been acquired. What Fritz eventually found out was that the particular style was a special favourite of the town's rougher element and not quite befitting of the Principal Teacher of English at Inverness Royal Academy.

Now, having turned away from those 84 years at the top of Stephen's Brae, we must make the two and a half mile journey to Culduthel for a brief,

Mirren Ramsay wins... Allan Beattie watches..... and Fred takes notes!

Sports Day '76

Bill Murray.... in charge as always on Sports Day

concluding insight into what the school has been like since the move.

The "flitting" of the summer of 1977 was even more hectic than the months of planning and preparation which preceded it as much of the contents of the Midmills building were transferred. In addition, courses for mixed ability first and second year classes - a completely new concept at Inverness Royal Academy - had to be prepared and many staff tuned into a fundamentally new way of thinking.

It was touch and go as to whether the new building would be ready in time, but once Jack McCall the Janitor decreed that it would, it simply had to happen.... and did. However the premises were still in some degree of chaos that August morning when around seven hundred pupils in the new S1-3 descended on the

In October Mr Alex. Munro retired after close on 28 years's valued service as the school's janitor. Mr Munro was appointed to the Academy staff in February, 1948. Over the years he earned the respect and affection of countless pupils. Sensible and just in dealing with any misdemeanors; kindly and helpful to those in need of advice and aid. To the staff, Alex. Munro was one of the school's best liked personalities, and a good friend. Always amicable and obliging, he was a fund of highly entertaining anecdotes which grew better and better with the passing years. We wish Mr and Mrs Munro a long and happy retirement in their new home at Braedown, Munlochy.

(1976 magazine)

place just 24 hours after several dozen staff had seen it for the very first time themselves.

It is traditional in a school that a new First Year have to rely on older pupils and staff to guide them from class to class for the first few weeks and this inevitably leads to some disruption. But here was a situation where more or less no one at all had the faintest idea of where they were going and the result for several days was complete chaos.

Fortunately the Culduthel building is relatively simple in layout with long corridors on three main floors. Each has an L shaped end for rooms to accommodate practical subjects and there are also ground floor music and PE departments. But it still took some time for everyone to find their way around.

In these days of modern technology, navigation about an unfamiliar building can be made easier by the "virtual tour". Such a photographic journey exists, at the time of writing in the summer of 1999, on the school's website, address:- **www.cali.co.uk/freeway/ira/virttour/free/index.html** At least this gives, among others, those who knew the old building a chance to inspect the new one at Culduthel, even from the other side of the world, a facility which unfortunately does not exist in the case of Midmills.

Among several new arrivals on the staff of what was now a much larger school was a sizeable contingent transferred from Millburn Secondary which had held around 500 pupils pending their entry into the Second and Third

Years at Culduthel. But although they were completely new in terms of the staffroom they actually had the advantage over their longer established colleagues because they knew a sizeable proportion of this mass of new pupils and had a good deal more experience of mixed ability teaching.

They were not, however, joined by Bill Murray who put in a week at Culduthel to complete his service and then retired, having done four years as an Assistant Rector following 23 as head of PE. There can be few staff who have identified so completely with the values and practices of the old set up at Midmills and Bill was more than prepared to admit that he really wanted none of Culduthel and was content to retire.

Soon Culduthel settled down and for the first two years until 1979 coexisted with Midmills on a split site basis. With assembly and registration fixed at the beginning of the day in the new premises and at the end in the old, a 15 minute time differential in one direction and 25 in the other were created between period starts to accommodate staff making the two and a half mile journey between the two buildings.

The late 70s was a period of extensive school building in Inverness and following the appearance of Culloden and Charleston Academies, the Royal Academy became one of five secondaries serving a town which less than 20 years previously had just two. The roll rose to a massive 1300 in the early 1980s before a variety of demographic factors caused a steady drop and it settled down at around 750 thereafter although it is now rising slowly again.

BATTLE HYMN OF THE I.R.A.

We lead our grim existence at the top of Stephen's Brae.
Our walls are cracked, and so are we, our critics often say.
We're getting old and crotchety, our hair is turning grey.
But we still go struggling on.

Glory, glory, what a terrible way to live!
Glory, glory, what a terrible way to live!
Glory, glory, what a terrible way to live!
But we still go struggling on.

Our Rector and his Deputy are losing all their hair,
The Heads of our Departments showing signs of wear and tear,
The Assistant Staff are killed with work, the kids—they just don't care.
But we still go struggling on.

Poor Leo in the language lab is twiddling knobs in vain,
And all the Frasers round the place are showing signs of strain.
While Annie in the music room is quietly going insane.
But we still go struggling on.

The colour scheme in Patsy's room, we really can't applaud.
Those startling reds and blushing pinks leave most folk over-awed.
And Walker's made a bloomer and electrocuted —.
But we still go sizzling on.

The Guidance Staff no longer work. They give advice instead.
And underneath the English books the kids have buried Ed.
And when you come to think of it, we might as well be dead.
But we still go struggling on.

ANON.

1976 Magazine

Gordon Harvey's drawing of the new Culduthel building 1977

And it is on that basis that the traditions of excellence, service and achievement, which have their origins in the first half of the 13th century, continue. The school's past surfaced in a major way at the Bicentenary in 1992 at which point many Invernessians probably found out for the first time that the Royal Academy actually started life in Academy Street.

Ian Fraser retired in 1993 whereupon John Considine became the twenty first Rector of Inverness Royal Academy. These days education is very different from earlier eras of major flagellations in the hall, the beating out of "dulce et decorum est pro patria mori" on the palm of the hand and the "presence" of D.J. at prayers in the old Midmills Hall. But it has been a process of constant evolution and despite the change of status and location, it is comforting to believe that those who were educated 'Up Stephen's Brae' can continue to feel some affinity with those of us who teach and learn these days at Culduthel.